When I Was Sifted

By

Cynthia Allen Curry

© Copyright 2006 Cynthia Allen Curry.

All rights reserved. No part of this publication may be reproduced, stored in a retrieval system, or transmitted, in any form or by any means, electronic, mechanical, photocopying, recording, or otherwise, without the written prior permission of the author.

Note for Librarians: A cataloguing record for this book is available from Library and Archives Canada at www.collectionscanada.ca/amicus/index-e.html
ISBN 1-4120-7304-9

Printed in Victoria, BC, Canada. Printed on paper with minimum 30% recycled fibre. Trafford's print shop runs on "green energy" from solar, wind and other environmentally-friendly power sources.

Offices in Canada, USA, Ireland and UK
This book was published *on-demand* in cooperation with Trafford Publishing. On-demand publishing is a unique process and service of making a book available for retail sale to the public taking advantage of on-demand manufacturing and Internet marketing. On-demand publishing includes promotions, retail sales, manufacturing, order fulfilment, accounting and collecting royalties on behalf of the author.

Book sales for North America and international:
Trafford Publishing, 6E–2333 Government St.,
Victoria, BC V8T 4P4 CANADA
phone 250 383 6864 (toll-free 1 888 232 4444)
fax 250 383 6804; email to orders@trafford.com
Book sales in Europe:
Trafford Publishing (UK) Limited, 9 Park End Street, 2nd Floor
Oxford, UK OX1 1HH UNITED KINGDOM
phone 44 (0)1865 722 113 (local rate 0845 230 9601)
facsimile 44 (0)1865 722 868; info.uk@trafford.com
Order online at:
trafford.com/05-2199

10 9 8

DEDICATION

*Dedicated to those who remained
as we suddenly found ourselves in the sieve.*

Stephen, for your faith, optimism, and ability to see beyond this world to one few could only imagine. Daylight is wonderful... I see the miracle in you, and yes, "God really does have it." Fantastic and getting better!

Stephcynie & Keith, my babies, my precious gifts from God. You endured so much but remained faithful to God, daddy, and me. I learned that wisdom has nothing to do with age. You are wise beyond "many" years. As you embrace the future, especially your own "suddenlies," never forget what you have already survived or what you are capable of overcoming. As I often tell you, "It is such a privilege being your Mom."

Mom & Dad, Claudette and Robert Eugene Edwards, for everything throughout my life. Thanks Mom for attending all those doctors and rehab appointments. I really did want you there. "Claude" I love you way too much, simply the best! "Daddy Dar" you are the greatest father in the world. And, according to your grandchildren, you two are the best grandparents on this planet! I certainly agree.

Cassandra Yvonne Adams, my incredible sister, ever present, no matter what...*From the cradle to the very end, my sister, definitely my dearest friend.*

Dottie Curry, for your love, concern and support. And, for everything great and small, thank you. We love you. May God enrich you in all things, in all ways, at all times.

Carlos Antonio Allen, words could never express my gratitude. I would not have made it without you. When I couldn't, you did with a kind spirit and a smile.

Barbara Harris, One who truly sticks closer than any sistah. Because of our friendship I get the bonus of having a "big dog prayer warrior," our Mom, **Miss Geneva Harris**. Blessings as God continue to shower you with supernatural favor.

Petite & Donnie McCowan, Jr., family first, friends forever. You listen, understand, never judge, and love unconditionally. I truly admire your life. "Are you sure we aren't sisters?" I think our grandmothers were on to something.

Kervin James, our "Ram in the bush." You have shown yourself faithful in all things. "Eyes have not seen what He has for you and yours."

ACKNOWLEDGEMENTS

Pamela Nichols, my sweet, beautiful, sister. When many forgot you remembered. For every kind deed, thought, action, and tear, thanks and many blessings.

Sylvia Harris, my CIA girlfriend. If I thanked you too much you would kill me. So, "Coffee later."

Pastors Marc & Delia Curry, your faith sustained us. You are a tremendous blessing to His Kingdom--uncompromising and unwavering in faith and belief. Many will enjoy their eternities because of you. Continue to live for His Glory (Deut. 28).

Bouquet Inc., the most powerful prayer warriors on planet earth! Mountains tremble at the sound of your voices. Angela Jones, Diane Milburn, Donna Wise Joseph, Honornell Sandling, Barbara Harris and Petite McCowan.

The Sandling's, Robert, Honornell, and adorable Laura for your unconditional love and support. Thank you **"Images to Remember Photography"** for the author's photograph.

Judith Jenkins, for your medical expertise, strength, advice, love, and wisdom.

Alva E. McNeal, for challenging me to fulfill my potential. Thank you for your input and suggestions on this manuscript, they are great.

James & Donna Joseph, ever-present, consistent and committed.

Anthony Curry, for just being Uncle Tony. God has a great future for you. Surrender and trust Him. He will not fail. (Jeremiah 29:11.)

Dr. Joe Samuel Ratliff, for the opportunity to learn, blossom and fly.

Adrienne Jennings, for the most genuine concern I've ever seen.

Randall Dobbins, Great relationships are based on God, integrity, and truth. Never compromise those and God will always reward you. You are "our younger brother." Your support, commitment, and friendship have always been a blessing.

Uncle Bennie & Nita, Mr. & Mrs. Conner JB Jones, for being our West Coast parents. We will always be grateful for everything.

Special Thanks

Danni Pruitt, Deborah Je'an, Nurse Bernie and Nurse Mark, Sherry Atkinson-Lively, Janice Workcuff, Miss Miola Laws, Willie Lane, Betty Stewart, Eredean Lyons, Mike and Glendora Chambers, and Dr. Virginia Mills. And to my family, Windsor Village U.M.C. under the awesome and dynamic leadership of Pastor Kirbyjon H. Caldwell (Pastor Suzette T. Caldwell), Pastor Velosia Kibe, BJ Traylor and the Transition Ministry team. The McGowens'—Gino, Kelly, Brandon, Cameron, and Corey.

For Prayers, Love, and Support

Pamela Hobdy, Nicole Stroud, Janae and Wanda Coleman, Willie Mitchell, Russell Kirkman, Aunt Betty Rose Price, Carmen Valentine, Vanessa Pratt, Gwendolyn Jones-Mitchell, Aunt Mary Jo and Uncle Eddie (Edwards),

Pamela D. Smith, Miss P ("Work It" Girl!), Scherra Jones-Bryant, Art Harris, Kathy Sapp, Rose Jordan, Miss Lucille Garrett, Micole Roy, Kathy Kelson, Willie Sylvester, Valda D. Page, Miss Dorothy Page, Reggie and Lisa Peppers, Miss Tena Davis, Josephine Johnson, Valencia Hardley-Turner, Joe Lee Allen, Helen Callier, Mrs. Kennedy, Mrs. Meisinger, Larry Curtis, Derek Curry, Connie Bennett, Jill Hopson, Yvette Johnson, Daryl Curry, Cedric and Chris Allen, Tia Bensen, Zachary Brown, Honorable Willie and Gwen Gauff. Emmanuel and Glory Okoro (Ivy), The Gibson's (Dottie and Rasheeda), The Westons' (Shakara), Patricia Bonner and The High School of Performing and Visual Arts Vocal Department (HSPVA), Margaret Russaw Caregivers Foundation, Inc., TIIR Challenge Program, and the Brentwood Baptist Church's Thursday Bible Class.

Lovingly
Michael Stephen Curry

And, My Wonderful Nieces, "You Are Such a Blessing"

Tiffany Nichols Curry, Tameka R. Orie, Wanoanah L. Adams, Crystalline S. Allen, and Victoria & Brienne Jennings.

Gone, But Never Forgotten, The Wonderful Memories Of

Lettie Mae Larkin (Maw Maw), Mae Dell Larkin Langston (Momma Mae), Ablee Silmon, Charles Raymond Langston (Pa Raymond), Mrs. Nancy Johnson (All time favorite teacher), Elean Phlgem (Aunt Miss), and Louise Jones.

To God Be the Glory....

Contents

Foreword 11

Introduction 13

Chapter 1
Wheat and Tears 17

Sifting is a process designed to turn your world upside down. No matter what life was like before, it will never be the same.

Chapter 2
...And Suddenly 28

"Suddenlies" are a series of unexpected, ongoing challenges, designed to "rock your world to its very core." They rarely come alone, but one after another, after another....

Chapter 3
Woe Is Me 50

Great change rarely occurs without trials. Setbacks are often setups for a better future.

Chapter 4
Brittle Stalk 102

The stakes are high for your defeat, but even higher for your victory. Special care is needed to sustain you during your dry and barren stage.

Chapter 5
The Shakedown 121

The shakedown forces you to walk the tightrope of life. Survival is not easy, but critical for your victory.

Chapter 6
Make Me Whole 130

The longer you are in the sieve, the greater your harvest potential. During the purification process, major losses occur. Most are necessary to propel you to your final destination.

Chapter 7
Lessons from the Sieve 138

Some of life's greatest lessons are learned from defeats, not victories. Some battles cannot be fought or won, simply endured. Lessons in the sieve are the foundation for restoration. Here, you begin to rebuild life.

Chapter 8
Harvestime 152

The final destination is where everything flows with ease. This is the place of extra and excess. Welcome to Harvestime.

Foreword

By
Barbara Harris-Curtis

I am always moved by the faithfulness of God in turning our painful trials into powerful testimonies. When I Was Sifted is a touching testament to God's amazing grace, tender mercy, and awesome power.

I am honored to recommend both the book and the author. Cynthia Curry is an extraordinarily gifted woman of God. I have been blessed by her friendship for over 30 years, during which time I have witnessed the consistent faith, strength, and endurance that have characterized the "sifting" seasons in her life. I thank God for leading her to share the life-changing truths she learned while "in the sieve."

Whether you are experiencing a major "sifting" or simply in need of an anchor to steady you through the storms of life, I pray that you will find encouragement and supernatural staying power in this God-inspired message of faith, hope, and restoration.

Blessings,
Barbara Harris Curtis
Author and Speaker

Introduction

By
Cynthia A Curry

"Simon, Simon, Satan has asked to sift you as wheat. But I have prayed for you Simon that your faith may not fail, And when you have turned back, strengthen your brothers." (NIV)

To God for the vision... Thank you, **Janice Workcuff**, author of <u>Road to Restoration</u> for the inspiration to forge ahead with this project. I treasure our sisterhood and admire your faith, strength, and tenacity. God has a great plan for you. Submit, release, trust, and follow Him. Be encouraged as you continue to inspire others. God has an exceptional track record and He will never fail you.

It is with great joy and humility that I present this book to anyone who has ever felt the despair of a hopeless, helpless situation. One, where there is no light, only darkness--the type of despair where if something does not happen you perish, when the only hope is a miracle. I have great news for you. God is still in the miracle working business. If you are at zero, you are a prime candidate for transformation. A simple touch from Him can change everything *in an instant.*

I do not profess to be a great writer but I hope these words will somehow encourage you to continue as you face your own shakedown. I believe they are inspired by one greater and hope you feel the same. By completing this, I have fulfilled a lifelong dream—to write a book. Somehow, in spite of it all, I managed to keep my dreams of a better future before me. Mine sustained me. I hope and pray that yours will too.

"A man without a dream will stay down, but show me one with a vision and I will show you one that no matter what always gets up." When I Was Sifted is a nine-year vision that for some reason, no matter how I tried, could never complete. It is one of at least three manuscripts I believe I will complete during my lifetime. Now I understand why it was clear in my head but never on paper.

Timing is everything and anything out of season is untimely. I had to be brittle, broken and purified. And, survive the shakedown before completing this process. The result is the fulfillment of a divine call to reach those who hurt. Although there are wonderful principles throughout this book that can be used by everyone, "sifting" is for those who know or have been exposed to Jesus in some way and at some time.

References to Satan are intentionally lowercased, my way of stressing his limited power. "Suddenlies" and "Shakedown" are inspired for this book and will become trademarks for future bodies of work I develop. References to wheat farming are not from experience but from reading and exploring the process which I find fascinating. Biblically, Matthew 13, and Amos 9:9, expound upon the principles presented here. Familiarity with the book of Job 1 and 2, are fundamental to understanding "the process."

As a woman, wife, and mother, The Holy Spirit revealed some things regarding Job, "the suffering book" from his wife's perspective. References to her are created to add substance to the story of a married family man who suddenly found himself in the sieve. My Biblical companion throughout this journey has been <u>The Comparative Study Bible</u> published by Zondervan Corporation.

Life is a beautiful journey, a series of challenges, changes, and new beginnings. Some I have endured, I would not wish upon anyone. This book is about getting through the trials of life so that you can fulfill your created purpose. When life "suddenly" change and force you to deal with unimaginable circumstances, trust God. He sustained me. And, I know beyond a shadow of a doubt He will sustain you.

My situation is nothing shy of a miracle. Hey, it is a miracle! If you are at the point of hopelessness, it is no coincidence that you chose this book. Or, maybe it chose you.... Read it, believe, and endure to the end. I'm praying that your faith does not fail.

Blessed Regards,
Cynthia A Curry

CHAPTER 1

WHEAT 'N' TEARS

Sifting is a series of unexpected "suddenlies," where some of the worse things you could *never* imagine happen. The process is designed to shake your world to its very core. Once started, theses *suddenlies* rarely come alone but in succession and in most instances without relief. Sifting is a season of huge mountains and giants. No matter what you do, they grow larger and stronger.

This season will challenge you like none other. It breaks you. There is little time to master or understand "the suddenlies" because as soon as one starts, another quickly follows. The process takes its course until life as you once knew it is never the same. Webster defines the word *sift* in the following manner:

> *To separate and retain the coarse parts with a sieve; to scatter or sprinkle through by means of a sieve; to examine closely; or to sort, scrutinize, inspect, search, probe. The sieve used for sifting is an instrument with a meshed or perforated bottom*

to separate coarse from finer parts. Sifting is when particles placed in the sieve are forced through for purification.

This author defines sifting as "forced purification" or a force that takes over your life placing you in unexplainable, uncontrollable situations that alter life, as you know it. Before the force, things were relatively normal. As a result of sifting, they will never be the same.

Although there are many harsh, unbearable trials throughout life, and none are discounted here, sifting is based on biblical principles designed to challenge your very being. Specifically, it is a battle for your faith in God. Sifting is most often reserved for, but not limited to God's finest. The greater your propensity to impact God's kingdom, the more likely you will suffer in the sieve.

A definite sign of a sifted season is sudden, unexpected, unexplainable losses. Losses you've never experienced nor could imagine. For instance, the sudden or tragic loss of a loved one, a relationship, or something you cherished. Sifting kept the Israelites in the wilderness for forty years and prevented Moses from getting into the Promise Land. Sifting caused Joseph a lifelong relationship with his family.

Job lost beloved children, health, home, wealth, and prestige. Hannah was barren and ostracized. David lost his firstborn. Ruth lost her homeland. Jacob lost his dignity; and, Jesus willingly gave the ultimate sacrifice, his life. In the end, all received greater rewards, but only after they suffered. In many ways sifting can be viewed as the defining moment of your faith walk. If there are solutions, like a parable, they seem hidden. During this season things are dry and barren.

Sifting will most likely occur at or near your most mature stage of Christianity or during some other challenging period of life. For example, as his ministry gained worldwide impact, the great Evangelist, Smith Wigglesworth experienced the sudden loss of his beloved wife. If you have *a call* on your life, you will eventually experience a period in the sieve. Security in your relationship with God makes you a prime target. Remember, Peter walked intimately with Jesus, but denied him three times.

Sifting is a battle for your faith or your potential greatness in God. Strategies against the attacks are futile because in some cases, the enemy has been allowed a period of time to wreak havoc in your life. So you can weather the storm, you think? Do not be deceived; the enemy has gone against bigger, better, seasoned, and stronger saints than you *and won*. Your job is to hold on to your faith at all cost. That will not be easy. You are wrestling with things beyond human comprehension.

You are wrestling with principalities, powers, rulers of darkness and spiritual wickedness according to Ephesians 6:10. In other words, the battle can not be won in the flesh. Human strategies are ineffective against the enemy who is older and wiser than time. God is the only one who can deliver you.

Speak to anyone with great impact for God's kingdom and most will tell of challenges they endured. When you are sifted the enemy will try to convince you that you are qualified to engage in combat with him. That is a tactical ploy to keep you distracted, a lie from old. Don't believe it. Without God, your arsenals of weapons are powerless. The enemy will inflict as much pain as possible, physically, mentally, and emotionally, to rob you of your faith.

> *"Suddenlies," a series of unexpected, ongoing, challenges that alter life as you know it.*

Depression and oppression will overtake you. You will suffer and experience losses like never before. Many friends and family may forsake you. Those who remain will not understand you or the season. Get ready to be lied on, questioned, abused, and embarrassed for seemingly no apparent reason. Confusion and chaos will become the norm, not the exception.

Sifting is the moment where *all-powerful meets limited power*. It is coming face-to-face with the adversary, the enemy of old, the devil. Sifting is a showdown where you are tested, broken, and tested again. The only way to win is to trust God. Remember, the enemy is older than time. You are no match for him without Christ. The outcome is already determined, but victory requires endurance. And, survival is often the hardest part of the season.

Unlike testing by your Heavenly Father who chastens, but remains compassionate, the enemy does none of that. He is more than happy to annihilate you. He is aware that he has a timeframe and must pull out the forces of hell to win. The devil does not just test; he wants to annihilate your dependency upon God. Since he was cast out of heaven, his goal has been to mock God.

According to Job Chapters 1 and 2, he walks the earth seeking whom he could destroy. He *got into* God's business for permission to sift you. He knew about your hedge and that he could not test you without permission. He looked at your righteous living, faith, and obedience and exercised his spiritual authority to make the request.

There has to be something great within to qualify for sifting. You have to be mighty special, a particular threat for a shakedown. Satan has exquisite taste preferring the very best. He does not request just anyone. He wants mature, strong saints, who can impact God's kingdom. Or, those saints who have yet to realize God's favor or anointing upon their lives. His mission is to minimize their impact within God's kingdom and abort their purpose. If he is successful, he assures that he can continue to fill the hollows of hell.

The enemy knows the lives you will impact. He also knows God's promises. The only way they will not manifest is if your faith fails. Getting a great saint in hell must be like a sinner coming to the Lord, a time to rejoice and celebrate. The lives and souls impacted are limitless. To destroy a great anointing comes at the expense of souls who would otherwise remain lost through eternity.

Heaven rejoices when the lost are brought to Christ; how much more would demons rejoice when a saint is brought down to the eternal fires of hell. Imagine, the bigger the saint, the greater the party. Don't be surprised if the devil does not have a special place in hell for fallen saints as a reminder to demons that persistence pays off. Imagine how hell would rejoice if great men and women of faith like Billy Graham, TD Jakes, Joel Osteen, Beth Moore, Creflo Dollar, Joyce Meyers, Charles Stanley,

Tony Evans, or *A God Chaser* like Tommy Tenny ended up there?

How about the chosen twelve, the disciples? Satan examined them and requested the one he felt had the strongest faith. Their lives greatly impacted the kingdom. For one to fall meant many would be doomed to hell. Thank God for their apparent hedge, but be assured that each was tested. Peter was specifically requested. Satan probably noticed him as he roamed the earth and requested to sift him.

Perhaps he wanted to sift them all, but God said one, test only one, any one you choose. Satan was given the opportunity to select from God's finest. Because of all that was at stake, the enemy must have carefully pondered his final selection. A wrong decision would limit the damage he could cause. Getting Peter to fall would be a bonus because of the souls he would ultimately impact for Christ.

A wise choice meant a new crop of souls that had yet to be harvested. He did not even consider Judas, because he was easy prey, but Peter's faith was firm. Satan must have looked over the disciples and determined to "maximize his moment." Then chose the one he felt had the most influence. The one he considered a major threat to his goal, filling the hollows of hell. Jesus had already said, "Upon this rock, I'll build my church," so, the enemy targeted Peter. He is no dummy. He knew Peter's very name meant rock or rock solid. To destroy the rock would certainly shake the foundation. Satan had to evaluate the odds and wage a bet that even though Jesus predicted Peter would be rock solid, if allowed, he could create such doubt that Peter would eventually denounce Christ and forfeit his anointing. On the other hand, Judas' very name meant traitor, a name that defined his nature. Satan did not even consider him. One of Webster's more interesting definitions of Judas is:

(Of animal) used as a decoy to lead other animals to slaughter. For example, a Judas goat is the goat the sheep followed to slaughter. They willingly followed because they had no clue of the dangers awaiting them.

Why bother with one who could be swayed? The enemy rarely wastes time on what he already has. But, winning Peter would be some party. Imagine the souls that would have been lost had Peter's faith failed. Imagine the sadness in heaven over those souls. When Jesus mentioned that Satan desired Peter, he did not call him Peter, but Simon and he said it repeatedly, as if to warn him.

Jesus knew what was inside of Simon Peter, but Peter had to find the rock solid faith within. Jesus could not give Peter faith. He had to acquire that on his own. He had to develop it to build the house God desired. Permission to sift Simon Peter was granted because God knew the outcome. Peter had to realize his greatness in Christ, but more importantly, Christ's greatness in him.

Simon had to suffer a shakedown until the rock emerged. In Luke, Chapter 22:31, Jesus told Peter, "Indeed, Satan has requested you, that he may sift you." Indeed is emphatic of satan's determination to have him. Jesus stressed that he prayed for him. Specifically Jesus said, "But I have prayed for you, that your faith should not fail; and when you have returned to me, strengthen your brother." Of course whatever Jesus says ultimately comes to pass, but before the manifestation, The Word is often tested. Jesus knew Peter would be victorious.

When the enemy wages war against you, it is to make you feel unworthy of the blessings that are rightfully yours. His goal is proving God wrong, mocking Him. Remember, the enemy has limited authority. When you are sifted, it may be difficult to remember that God is All-sovereign, but even then, some areas of your life remain off limits. Sometimes you will recognize them, other times you may not until the process is complete.

Perhaps the hardest part of sifting is the lack of control. Sifted living is unpredictable forcing you to live moment to moment. Attacks do not cease. In most cases, things become worse before getting better. Permission has been granted and the process must be completed.

Mature saints must be humorous in the sieve. The enemy is especially prepared for them. He knows most will rely on prayers and faith, the very thing that is being tested. He smiles as they seek God. Satan knows that humans are no competition for him. He chuckles at attempts to survive, and pokes fun of their ability to utilize natural means to resolve supernatural situations.

He knows spiritual laws that most are unaware of and could never have privy to without the aide of the Holy Spirit. So, he distracts with more "suddenlies." The enemy knows that human beings can only understand human things. He knows that if you understood supernatural laws, you would not be in your predicament.

Knowing that God has somehow allowed the season is of little comfort. Like Job and "Mrs. Job" you would not wish your experience upon anyone. How could God grant permission and abandon you to such a state when you have been so faithful? Yet, Job 1:9-13, 2:4-6 and Luke 22:31-32, specifically illustrate that permission is granted in advance.

One of the first lessons is sifting is a process that separates good from bad; pure from impure; and, holy from unholy. God needs uncontaminated saints. Although Peter was a great saint, before he could fully walk in his purpose, he had to be tested and refined. When the devil asked Jesus for Peter, he seemed to mockingly say:

Peter is no rock; he is not even quick sand. How can you use him to build your church? If you would remove that hedge for a moment, I'll show you what he is made of and it is certainly not rock. Instead, try sinking sand or better yet quick sand. There is little structure or security in that one. I can't believe you want him to head up the church. You are wrong this time. I can easily destroy him if you would just remove that hedge. Besides, if he is so solid, let me place him in the sieve and shake him up.

You will be sifted where you are strongest, passionate, influential, or in areas close to your heart. You may also be sifted in areas that hinder your spiritual growth. If you wrestle with pride, are self-centered, expect a period in the sieve. Satan was hurled out of heaven because of that. God cannot use proud, self-centered people who hinder kingdom building. God cannot fully operate in your life until you completely surrender. Through Him you find strength to accomplish things you never could in your own right.

Still, Gethsemane is a place where even the strongest saints feel forsaken. Humans can only comprehend so much when it comes to spiritual things. The great news is that once the process is over, you will be free from contaminants that hinder your walk or others. God's thoughts are not yours. Expect your understanding to be limited. To paraphrase Christopher Reeves (Superman) who once said in an interview about his tragedy, "If I could not handle it, it would not have happened to me."

God grieves as you are sifted and especially when you cry out, but because He formed you, He knows what you can handle. As the Father, He must hesitate to grant permission, but just as laws rule the earth, they also rule heaven. Once the cycle starts, spiritual laws operate and the process must run its course. The potter who formed you knows everything about you including your limitations.

Your situation may be beyond comprehension but God understands every aspect of your struggle. He is making changes that will last a lifetime. God knows impurities must be removed to refine you. The fiery furnace will bring forth your brilliance. He knows what has to come out to birth what is inside. God who formed you is always with you. He knows how to sustain you and has made every provision as you approach the shakedown. The ultimate goal is to be molded in the image of Christ.

Sifting produces a testimony that convicts and becomes the hallmark of your greatness in God. Sadly, the season is marked with pain, despair, and hopelessness. You do not get through the sieve unscathed. Sifting is not like other difficult periods. You may be forced to experience another suddenly as you wait for deliverance from the present one. The changes are not designed to slay you, but strengthen you. Losing is not an option. You lose, but losses will be necessary in order to gain God's promises.

Sifting creates new hunger, thirst, trust, and love for Him. The result is a new improved life with zeal for God. Sifting leaves no doubt that something "life altering" occurred. Everything and everyone around you will be touched in some way. In the end God restores, and in most instances gives more. As you survive your suddenlies, remember Jesus has already made provisions for you to succeed. Flesh cannot withstand a spiritual shakedown. But, God specializes in them. Stay focused on Him, so that your faith will not fail.

Chapter 2

...AND SUDDENLY!

Flip through the pages of the Bible, it is clear that those who did great work for the kingdom were sifted. Human beings can never prepare for it, because sifting is spiritual. When the faithful are suddenly forced through the sieve, they are naturally confused. Serving in the kingdom comes with certain benefits, including God's hedge. But, there is often a greater hidden cost. The enemy must petition God and God must grant permission for sifting. Once granted, spiritual laws override natural ones.

There are many Biblical examples of sifted saints, like Job, Peter, Hannah, Moses, and Joseph. In Amos Chapter 9:9-15, the house of Israel is referred to as being sifted or separated. And, Matthew Chapter 13, explains the principal of sowing and reaping; and, separating wheat and tares. This book defines sifting as "forced purification" or a force that takes over your life placing you in unexplainable, uncontrollable situations that alter life, as *you know it.* What separates a sifted season from other harsh ones is it is *a battle for your faith.*

Regardless of your faith level, walk, or relationship with God, sifting is the harshest trial you will ever face. The devil is perfectly aware that he has a specific timeframe. He is also aware that you are out of your league. He knows the season must run its course according to the time allocated by God. Since the devil is "on the clock," one of his first strategies is attacking your mind.

A self-defeatist mentality takes you out of the game before the battle begins. The enemy knows that "As a man thinks, so he shall be." Weakening

> *Simon, Simon behold, Satan has demanded permission to sift you as wheat...*
> (Luke 22:31 NAS)

your mind makes his job easier. Once you believe his lies, he is halfway there with little effort. Hold your mind captive to the things that are not of God. He is your only chance to survive.

When you are sifted, low moods are common. Take authority over them. Seek God and cast out fear, doubt, isolation, unbelief, grief, anger, and guilt. Those emotions weaken the mind. And, a feeble mind is easy prey. Since the enemy does have "some" authority in the spiritual realm, there are things he understands that cannot be comprehended by natural means.

There are some things that can only be revealed by the Holy Spirit; but, if your mind is distracted, you can never focus on them. Since you do not know why you have been singled out, you cannot engage in an effective counter attack without the aid of the Holy Spirit. The enemy wants you bound by your circumstances to distract you from God. In the Book of Job the devil roamed the earth then presented himself before God, along with the other Angels. There he requested to sift Job.

The mere fact that he was among the "Sons of God" indicate he has rights and inside knowledge of spiritual matters we are not privy to in the natural. Imagine, satan can appear before God when in the natural, we cannot? In John 16:11, Jesus calls him, "The prince of the air and ruler of the world." Rulers are organized, influential, strong, powerful, and possessive. They have inside access to sensitive information, weapons, people, places, and things.

Rulers are resourceful and extremely possessive about territory. They will destroy anyone or anything that threatens it. You are a threat to the enemy's territory. That is why you have been targeted. There may be other reasons, but you are a "force to be reckoned with."

When there is an anointing on your life, expect a season in the sieve. Satan desires to control the world and everything in it and that means you. Your very potential is a threat. He wants to annihilate you. The test is for you to learn what is inside. It provides insight into your strengths and weaknesses. It helps you recognize God's power in your life.

No matter how hopeless your situation, God promises hope for a better future. You may not understand how the enemy works, but God certainly does. He wants you to persevere at all costs and develop child-like trust in Him. Look to Him for your way out. God use adversities and trials to bring you to greater levels in Him. Satan wants to kill, steal and destroy your potential. But, God, not the devil chooses the sifting process. He set the parameters. During each phase, trust Him to sustain you.

No one gets through life without trial or tragedy. Still everyone is not chosen for sifting. Sifting is for those who have had or have a relationship with God. It is based on Biblical principles, designed to test your faith. Luke Chapter 22, along with the Book of Job is the basis for these thoughts. Additionally, Amos Chapter 9 and Matthew Chapter 13 explain these principles.

The most important thing about sifting is it is spiritual. Sifting separates things that hinder God's work in your life. The more intimate the relationship the greater the tests. When you are sifted, but unsaved or backslidden God may be trying to get your attention and draw you to Him.

Maybe you have made mistakes like the prodigal son, who was indecisive, undisciplined, and impulsive desiring a worldly life instead of one of promise. He even attempted to justify his hog pen situation. Well God is waiting with open arms, like his father to welcome you home. He understands his creation. He knows comfort zones are preferred and unless challenged most will never achieve their full potential. Through his trials, the prodigal son made a decision that changed his life forever. Your trials will also redefine you.

Growth is the key to maturity in the kingdom. God allows trials as opportunities for long-term change. Change, though uncomfortable, force decisions that may otherwise be discounted. God is fully aware of your struggles but understand the process necessary to develop your unique gifts. Instead of bad seeds, He knows only the best will remain. He is not concerned about the end result because the battle has already been won.

God will use the season to mold you into the vessel that is most effective for the call on your life. "His will, not yours." He wants holy and righteous seeds especially when your life influences others. Pastors and spiritual leaders are an example of this. Their influence over their congregations is significant. With churches reaching numbers in the thousands, today's "mega churches" and their leaders often wield more power than many Fortune 500 CEO's. Imagine that kind of power in the hands of one who has not dealt with their sin.

Many "mega leaders" are viewed and treated as celebrities. Those who do not spend ample time before the throne could easily fall prey to the hype, and begin to believe their success is a result of their own genius, ingenuity or power. The result is reprobate behavior--accepting abnormal behavior as normal when it specifically contradicts Biblical principles. Personal motives over pure and holy ones create unhealthy congregations that are misfed and mislead. Whenever a religious leader desensitizes to sin, they attract and breed flocks that embrace and overlook it.

Whether religious, secular, or in the home, leaders set the tone for their organizations. Those who tolerate sin create organizations that do the same. Enron is a modern day example of this. Skilled leaders refused to create systems of checks and balances to protect the ones who relied upon them most. Their insensitivity destroyed many lives. The results are still being felt. Greed and power does that. Religious leaders can also have that kind of impact, good or bad.

Those who justify sin, pimp, or prostitute God's anointing will be accountable through eternity. Those with the gift of leading souls must be beyond reproach. With all that is at stake, God cannot entrust great anointing to just anyone. Leaders must be holy and acceptable before the Lord. They are often envied but those who envy them could never withstand the pressure of being in their position.

God knows the greater the saint, the more opportunity to choose sin. With everything at their beck and call it is easy to fall into temptation. Since no one is perfect, those with particular "isms" must stay before the throne to remain pure. You are one of God's leaders. Your sphere of influence might not be as large, but you have one. The enemy would rather you not know that. That is why it is important to survive.

Suddenlies

Sometimes a person does not know what he is made of or what he can survive without *suddenlies*. They are the physical change associated with sifting, events that are beyond comprehension. They alter life, as you know it. *Suddenlies* can be compared to a natural disaster whose effects are felt for years beyond the catastrophic occurrence. Previously you may have known others to experience them but never in a million years could you imagine *it* happening to you. Now it is your turn to face the challenge of a lifetime.

Sifting is a series of *suddenlies* that seem endless. A series of challenges that force you to live your own worse nightmare or horror movie, except it is real. You are the main character, the star with top billing. Sifting causes man to seek God like never before. Perhaps the only good thing about it is God allows it. This is your life. You must fight to keep it. There is seemingly no rhyme, ration or reason for the attacks.

Suddenly your life collapses, you wonder what has happened. Suddenly, your loved one is killed in a car crash or murdered at the hand of another. Suddenly, your child walks out of the door, never to be seen again. Suddenly, a trusted sitter or worse, a relative, molests your innocent child. Suddenly, as you go along your day you are assaulted, robbed, beaten or raped. Suddenly, your healthy love one dies for no apparent reason. Suddenly, you find yourself in a life changing health crisis.

You are diagnosed with terminal lung cancer, though you never smoked. In fact, you are a "health nut," but suddenly, your annual check up reveals cancer, full-blown AIDS, or worse. Suddenly, things you once took for granted are gone. That job or business you believed God for, the one that provided for your family, failed leaving you penniless.

Suddenly, your spouse of thirty years reveals an affair or a secret lifestyle. Suddenly, you find out that the outstanding child you raised is a drug addict or worse. Suddenly, life savings and retirement are gone. Or suddenly, you find yourself pregnant with the child of your dream. After a stellar pregnancy and labor, the child is still-born. These are some examples of *suddenlies*. They are the hallmark of a sifted season.

At times, staying sane is insane. Simple things require all your energy. In most instances all you can do is hold on. Where is God and what allowed Him to grant permission? You are being tested. Instead of peace, *suddenlies* challenge your very core. It seems that God cannot be found, but like a professor, who is silent during a test, He remains quietly in the room. Prior to testing the professor lectures, answers questions, and provides ongoing input; but, once the test starts, you are on your on. It is up to you to figure out the correct answers.

He remains quiet because he is confident of your ability. God is always nearby. He applauds as you master each lesson. He knows the suffering does not compare to the glory that is in store. At times, He would love to step in and save you but that would hinder the process. So, when you are sifted, tolerance, patience and waiting become your friends. In due season, you reap, cope, and live. God never fails and the outcome is always for the greater good. That is a theme throughout this book. God never fails.

Choices

God may allow sifting in areas where your knowledge is limited or where you need growth or change. Or, in areas where you are naturally gifted or have already experienced great success. He may allow sifting to change weaknesses into strengths; immaturity to maturity; or, to deliver you from a sin filled life. Saints long to rationalize and get relief, but rarely do. Sifting could be the result of many things, especially pride. Pride and selfishness almost always summon a season in the sieve. Both are definite areas that hinder a good crop.

Sifting could result from poor choices. Bad decision making can create generational problems including, low faith, low self-esteem, deception, depression, envy, slothfulness, hatred, jealousy or addiction. *Goody-two-shoesism*, perfectionism, and *know-it-all ism* are pride driven. Meanness, timidity, fear, and stubbornness are barriers that attract havoc. They make it easier for the devil to operate. Add to that lack, greed, lust, materialism or elitism and blinders are created that mask God's vision for your life.

Sometimes just being connected to someone who makes poor decisions can alter your life, especially within families. If someone close to you is sifted, you will feel the affects. For example, children are under the authority of their parents or caregivers. Unhealthy parents can create unhealthy children. Things as basic as choosing the proper neighborhood or school could greatly impact a child's future. Or, something simple like placing the child's need first can make a lasting impression.

Some parents never realize that basic truth. Many are unwilling to sacrifice for anyone. Then children have no choice about the way they live. They are forced to overcome bad choices and circumstances with little assistance. Once they become adults, many never look back. Sadly, sifting can force you to leave those who are unwilling to change. Regardless of the circumstances, with God, you can overcome your past as long as you have a glimmer of hope.

Poor decisions may hinder or delay destiny but does not have to destroy it. Start where you are. Turn your situation over to Him. Let Him give you divine wisdom for a new start. Suddenly, new meaning is found within your struggle. Still, sifting could be the result of a time and a season appointed by God.

When you are sifted, one thing is certain; life is never the same. Through grace, God continues to protect you as you strive toward your destination. Once you survive, use what is in you hand to restructure your life. When you experience a series of *suddenlies,* there is probably a great anointing on your life, something that can transform and benefit others. Sifting brings out a convicting testimony.

"All In the Family"

The story of Jacob is a great example of a family who was sifted because of poor choices. The family's sin was deception. Because of a mother's bad advice to her son, they suffered for years. Jacob's story is filled with betrayal. His very name meant trickster, deceiver. He inherited generational proclivities from his mother, Rebekah and refined them working for her brother Laban. The wages of sin is death and one sin does ripple and affect the lives of others, especially within families. Generational sins provide the enemy easy access.

What a tragedy, an entire family betrayed each other for a blessing that would have gone to Jacob anyhow. To preserve his life, Jacob was separated from his family and suffered years of abuse, mistreatment, and deception at the hands of his Uncle Laban. Ultimately, he received new life and fulfilled God's purpose, but not until he was sifted. Jacob learned that blessings could not be based on lies. The saddest part of the story is mother and son never saw each other after the deception. Rebekah died before Jacob returned.

Circumstances overshadow God's promises. Manipulation is sometimes used to counterfeit genuine blessings. Before Jacob could return home, he had to be sifted, processed, and purified. Facing his twin brother after the betrayal demonstrated the humility that Jacob learned while he was away. He learned that when God allows sifting, it is to give you something, not to take something away. Imagine as he matured, worked, and was deceived, he became tired of his ways. He had to learn that everything he wanted was already his. He received that promise at birth. Something his mother apparently forgot to tell him that could have made all the difference in the family's history.

Jacob desired life without limitations and yearned for one based on truth. He chose to break the curse that bound him and his family. He recognized that he could not get a legitimate blessing without a Godly encounter. He faced the inevitable. Perhaps he knew a wrestling match would force him to rid himself of things that hindered his potential. As tough as it was, a victory assured a legitimate blessing. He came to understand that "what God had for him, was his."

Jacob took the long route to his blessed place, but you do not have to maneuver and manipulate for yours. If God promised some things, expect them. If sifting is needed to obtain them, endure it. In the end, it will be worth it. His word cannot return void. What is ordained can never be changed. Whatever happens on the journey is necessary to end up in your blessed place.

When you are at zero, devoid of hope, God provides to let you know He is near. He knows your history, but He also knows your future. He knows the entire story. Unlike your version where there is probably some excitement, consistency, and gradual change, with few challenges and a predictable ending. When God writes it, the story changes moment to moment.

His version is like an "Indiana Jones" encounter, stepping from one adventure to another. Impossible and hopeless situations create suspense to captivate the audience. God allows you to be the main character because He knows you have what it takes to make it to the end of the story. God is the greatest storyteller of all time. His stories are episodic in proportion. Humans could never conceptualize the beginnings or endings. With God it is finished means things have just begun. Endings are often new beginnings.

Those who thought they knew the story are amazed at the twists and turns, screaming scenes and impossible situations, yet you survived. In God you live happily ever after. The story is not just for you but His glory. And like any great story, they are not as exciting when you know the ending. No one would stick around to finish if they knew the outcome. God will make sure they read your book, watch your movie, or play your video game. The outcome is amazing. Blessings may be harder to identify, but they are there. Blessings are for you, but miracles are for characters within or connected to the story.

Miracles are for unbelievers and the ones who thought you wouldn't make it. Those who wanted you to give up and thought you lost your mind. In the end, even they will have to admit a greater power sustained you. Since you have probably experienced them before, the nonbelievers, doubters, or "haters," who have never experienced them will see God's power operating in your life.

How will those watching know God moved if it looks like you did it yourself? Remember, satan only requests the finest. He desires saints like Peter and ones like you. Satan requested Peter for the ultimate shakedown. Permission was granted and the wrestling match began. Notice, the shakedown began after Jesus warned Peter.

The Holy Spirit often nudges when something is not right. Perhaps prior to your sifting you noticed something. Maybe you felt that something was not right. Or felt a vexation like the one I felt one morning when my entire family took a fate filled trip. Had I stopped immediately and prayed in the Spirit for revelation knowledge, maybe spiritual help could have minimized the damage.

Although nothing can avert God's will when He ordains a thing, prayer can powerfully affect the outcome. Prayer positions you to deal with suddenlies. As close as he was to the Lord, Peter must have thought that even if the devil desired him, because of his intimate relationship, knowledge, and faith, he would never deny Christ. Peter probably thought, "I am Pete, the rock, ready to withstand any attack." The one even you said you would build your church on. As Peter denied Christ, He looked straight into his eyes. He must have felt condemnation, failure, disappointment, and guilt. But, Jesus looked into his eyes, not to condemn, but to remind him that his faith would not fail.

As a result of being sifted, Peter was entrusted with a great task for the kingdom, including writing portions of the New Testament. Most could not withstand what it took to be in his shoes. He was a chosen vessel. God knew he would be rock solid. He is among an "A list" of those who survived the shakedown, including Moses the murderer, Paul the persecutor, Rahab the prostitute, David the adulterer, and Jacob the deceiver. Like them, "the devil desires to sift you, but just like them, your faith will not fail.

"RSVP"

Job was also requested for sifting. Throughout mankind, there is probably no one who experienced the harsh trials he endured. Satan's reason was that he was righteous and had God's hedge. Prior to the request, his life seemed perfect. God even boasted of his righteousness. Yet, *suddenly*, his life took a turn for the worse. Job could not possibly imagine losing *everything*.

Like many attempting to serve, God's righteous servant found himself in quite the predicament. Job lost beloved children, houses and land. He endured alienation, gossip, despair, lies, hurt, pain, loneliness, illness, depression, and brokenness. Family and close friends denounced him as a fool and insinuated that he somehow caused his maladies. Friends tried to get him to agree that God would not allow any righteous man to suffer that way.

Job maintained that God would deliver him. He endured. During the process, certain components remained off limits, including Mrs. Job, who told her husband to "curse God and die." She suffered the same losses and is often portrayed as the negative part of sermons on his life. During the climatic presentation, it is always cited that she instructed her husband to curse God. Realistically her emotions better portray how most would behave given the same set of circumstances.

In extreme crises, many mature saints question God, and yes, even curse him. If you have been in intimate fellowship with him, imagine the guilt. Mrs. Job was at the end of her rope and could not see reasons to continue to serve a God who would allow such hardships. She was more the norm than the exception. Thankfully, during those difficult days, she remained under the covering of her husband who refused to give up on God. Prior to the request, Job experienced much favor--beautiful children, houses, land, cattle, etc. According to scripture, Job could not experience that kind of favor without Mrs. Job.

Scripture says, "He who finds a wife, finds a good thing and obtains favor from the Lord." (Proverbs 18:22). Favor is what God uses to build an abundant life. Much of his favor was probably the result of her faithfulness, prayers, and wisdom. While Job was away making all those business deals, she made sure everything was in tact on the home front. She assured that when he went into meetings he was dressed in the finest fabrics. She probably made most of his suits. She gave wise counsel on many of his business deals and even warned him of those who did not have his best interest at heart.

Like many dynamic women, she had her own business. By all accounts and from his abundant lifestyle, Mrs. Job was probably the consummate Proverbs 31 woman who found herself in a situation beyond human comprehension. There is a saying that "There is no loss like that of a child." Imagine, she conceived, carried, birthed, and lost ten children. Certainly, no woman could imagine surviving that! Add to that lost home, land, cattle, wealth, savings, retirement, social status; and, the defiled state of her "righteous" husband. Well, you get the picture. Perhaps you would curse God, or at least think about it. Maybe you already have.

Her statement exemplifies extreme depression. The most severe stage is suicide or in her case to "Curse God and die." At that time, she had no idea that her husband could not be restored without her assistance. Somehow Job maintained his conviction. He would not allow anyone to define him by his present condition. He believed that God was still God. Maybe he knew he was being tested. His wife, through her pain, lost sight of that.

Job's ability to hold on assured that she would also be restored. Seeing her in such a pitiful state was probably as hard as the physical suffering he endured. Job probably reflected on the joy of finding her. Oh, the joy she must have brought to him and their children. She must have been a wonderful wife and mother. She had to be beautiful in form, in tip-top shape to conceive and birth ten healthy children. She must have been amazing but the wear of the season robbed her of that. Like most women, she was probably the rock of the family.

She encouraged him when he failed, made mistakes, or lost favor in the gates. While he was away working, she taught the children the things of God. She prepared them for church, mid-week Bible Study, washed and mended their clothes, bought and prepared food, and made sure bills were paid in a timely manner. Whether or not saints openly admit it, most have questioned or perhaps cursed God. Saints put on a great public face, but the private anguish is often unbearable.

If you have ever said, "Why me Lord," then you have had a "Mrs. Job moment." God understands human emotions and knows the process needed to get through the difficult periods. Instead of feeling guilty, God knows you are only human. He forgives, totally and completely and loves you no matter what.

You might not be as strong or faithful as Job. Maybe you have already cursed God and harbor the guilt it brings. Aha, the enemy has you right where he wants you. God knows your heart and how fragile you are during the shakedown. You have everything you need to get through the sieve. Remember, at one point Jesus even said, "My father, why have you forsaken me." You might wonder, what is the point? Why continue to strive, trust, and believe God? As far as you can see He actually abandoned you.

> *Zero, the place where miracles occur!*

There is great news for you, even when you give up on God; He never gives up on you. In your weakest moments, God is there. Maybe you are at zero, where the story takes on episodic proportions, where no one sees the ending. God is preparing you. He wants the good kernels inside to survive.

How would you know what you are made of if it were not for the sieve? How strong could your witness be without it? You must understand your greatness in God and

His power in you. Zero is the best place for miracles. How can your testimony be strong enough to save or impact others when you are unable to save yourself? The glory is in the story. The potter who created you knows every crack. He knows your capacity.

The enemy wants to weigh you down with the cares of the world. Anything else that can go wrong, he'll make it happen. Expect to become "sick and tired of being sick and tired," but never give up. "Microwave solutions" may seem easy, but complete the process and allow the pain to work out the impurities. Forget worldly antidotes like drugs, alcohol, gambling, illicit sex, pornography, negativity, pills, compulsive shopping, doubt, criticism, murmuring, complaining, gossip, etc. Do not take the easy route and please do not "idolize" your problem by putting more emphasis on it than God. Don't let your temporary circumstances define your long-term destiny. Trust God not your circumstances. Even when you can no longer run, stay in the race. In your weakest moments, He is there.

Stay strong. Obtain your promise. "The battle is not yours. You are more than a conqueror, and yes, can do all things." You are blessed. Rise above your situation. Jesus has already dethroned the enemy. Victory is assured. Fight or better yet stand until the season is over. When your faith seems to fail is exactly when Jesus goes before the Father, interceding for help that arrives in the nick-of-time. The enemy desires to kill you, but God wants to bless you.

Bid your blessed season to come forth. Survival is crucial to your blessing. Remind yourself that Jesus has already prayed. Your faith cannot fail! No matter how difficult, God will deliver you. Stay in the race. "Fight the good fight of faith." Even if you are wounded you will not perish.

Right now, you might be in your own Gethsemane, but God is faithful. The season is part of a divine plan. Search your soul. Ask the hard questions. Maybe you need stretching before "He expands your territory." Perhaps the faith you have is not strong enough for where God is taking you. Maybe you are even a saint with little or no real power?

Pray and correct areas that could hinder your breakthrough. If you need to make amends, do it. If there is someone you need to forgive, act fast. Do your part. God will do His. Clean out your emotional house. Toss everything that is not beneficial. Maybe you need to clear out your physical space, "de-clutter." Give and throw out things you no longer need. If you are being sifted financially, don't expect God to bless you if you do not follow His spiritual laws.

Increase your tithes or at least give your 10%. No matter how much or how little you receive, always give God the required tenth. Don't try to rationalize that you cannot afford to tithe. If you are going through financially, you cannot afford not to! If it is not enough for your need, use it for a seed. Missing it here will create additional problems that will cost more than you are willing to pay. Besides, God does much more with the 10% than you could ever do with the 90% He allows you to keep. If you haven't tried tithing, do it and trust Him to meet your needs.

Volunteer for a worthy cause or something that you are passionate about. If unsure, the area you are being sifted in might be a good place to start. Spend more time learning about God. Learn to hear and follow His voice, not yours. Trust God to handle His part. Seasons are great, because good or bad, they always change.

Be wary of the advice of friends who have not "walked in your shoes." They might love you but their advice will be based on their perspective, ideals, and feelings about your circumstances. A person can hardly give sufficient advice in an area they have not personally experienced or had success in. When your season has gone on too long; they will offer ways out when God is offering you a way through. They may also want you to justify things you've done wrong or should do differently. Their advice will be endless.

Job's good friends thought no one could be in his predicament unless they did something. Yours will discount your innermost convictions in lieu of theirs. Their opinion of your situation is all that matters—to them. They will convince themselves and sometimes you, that you are not rational enough to make good decisions. Seek God and continue to follow Him especially when things are hard. If unsure, He will confirm His word. In most cases your inner voice already knows His will. Trust that sound.

Even those with great faith may attempt to rationalize spiritual matters with a natural mindset. But, there is nothing natural or rational about what you are going through. The only reason you survived so far is because of supernatural, not natural means. Right now, you might not see God, but He is near. Allow him to develop survival strategies and the grace to implement them. Grace is given for even basic, little things like grocery shopping, which in extreme situations need a strategic plan. There is always "a ram" for the greatest need. "Rams" are things that are available to meet urgent needs.

Maybe a trusted friend shows up bearing the exact thing you need. That is an example of a ram. Or, a neighbor decides to cut your grass for weeks on end. Other friends collaborate with random acts of kindness. And, a simple cup of coffee, a friendly outing, or a listening ear can lift your spirit. Perhaps there is that brave individual that invites your entire family for dinner. Maybe someone else sends passes to a movie, play, or a gift certificate for a long overdue manicure or haircut. And, my favorite is someone calls saying they were thinking of and prayed for you. Those are all "little rams" that God uses to keep you going.

Friends who remain even if they do not understand provide a sense of normalcy during a consistently abnormal period. You appreciate things once taken for granted. Simple things like a restful night's sleep, a home, lights, hot water, and air condition are blessings. Once sifted, you never overlook a real need, when it is in your power to help. There is no choice but to fill it. You have been sifted and know that it is not about you, but about God's power through you.

The seed you sow could be the one that bears fruit. Though it might seem small, every kind deed is a great seed. Purchase some mustard seeds if necessary. Carry them around to remind you of their potential and yours. Take "one" out and see how tiny it is. With the naked eye, it is barely visible, yet that seed produces one of the greatest plants imaginable. If you drop one, the chances of finding it is virtually impossible, but God can easily locate it. God sees your faith, even if it is weak. He can locate the tiniest seed and find the great one. He can manifest the largest blessing of your life. Your job is to stand or withstand until "it is finished." And, "suddenly," just as quickly as the season began, it ends.

Find a set of memorial stones, victories from seasons when blessings flowed (Joshua 4:1-7). Remind yourself of what He has already brought you through. Write down and recount past victories. They will strengthen you to keep going. Jesus is praying that your faith does not fail.

CHAPTER 3

Woe Is Me

She was mild, lovely, gentle and kind, but she was no average grandmother. "She was something else." Her most endearing quality was her ability to see the good in all things and people, no matter what. She believed everyone, and I mean everyone, was beautiful. She was full, round and robust. Her face carried a trademark smile that was uniquely hers. Her skin was firmer than the average forty year old, though she was approaching seventy.

She loved cooking almost as much as she loved eating. She was meticulously clean. For example, even though there was hot, running, water in her country home, she boiled water to sterilize everything, including her toothbrush, everyday. Unlike many grandmothers of her era, she went to college on an academic scholarship. Since her father was a railroad worker, she took advantage of the opportunity to travel and explore the world, free of charge.

To say she was adventurous is an understatement. She thought that the world should be seen and experienced. She had a baby out of wedlock, her only child, in her day a definite taboo. Oh, she eventually married, but in her own time, on her own terms. Her daughter was almost five when she stood as flower girl in their wedding. By then, rumors had subsided and everyone seemed to be over the shame of a daughter getting pregnant and refusing to marry, although her father insisted that she did. Of course having an adorable first grandchild helped ease the shame. She would be her only child, the light of everyone's eyes.

Although she was always in our lives, my first conscious memories of her were probably around age three. As a young child, I remember that she was always busy preparing things in the kitchen or doing various chores throughout the house. She would often go out to the garden, planted and maintained by her mother, my great-grandmother, to pull fresh greens, purple hull peas, and the like. Their modest property was filled with fruit trees and various things a child could enjoy. Their small wood framed house had a beautiful *picture window* that seemed much larger from my childhood eyes.

There were apple trees that bore the sweetest fruit one could imagine, and the pear trees yielded an unending harvest that everyone in the community partook of. To sell any of these delicacies would break the code of giving that both my grandmother and great-grandmother lived by. In addition to pears and apples, there were apricot, fig, peach, plum, and pecan trees. During summer visits these served as wholesome snacks. Both my grandmother and great-grandmother would *can* every summer.

There was never a shortage of pear or peach preserves, canned vegetables, and the like. I watched as they stirred ingredients in huge kettle pots to create sweet and healthy sensations we would enjoy throughout the year. Since my great-grandmother and most of her siblings lived to ripe old ages, I had the privilege and pleasure of having both a granny and a great-granny. As a child, I thought this was normal and could not imagine it any other way. Little did I know this was definitely the exception. My grandmothers were unlike "nouveau grannies" today. Grandmothers back then were old, ancient, a requirement. Today, she could easily be in her forties and younger.

Both had children late for their era. I adored my great-grandmother and thought her to be one of the most fascinating women I'd ever encountered. She taught me many things about life, not through words, but by her actions. She had the strongest constitution ever, and I have yet to experience anyone else like her.

I often remember her on bended knees, huge, black, Bible in hand wailing. As a young child I could not understand her need to be there so often or so long. As a woman, I came to know that the stoic, quiet, strong, and proud woman I adored found strength to endure her *suddenlies* there. Suddenlies, I am certain were the hallmark of the unwavering faith she demonstrated throughout her life.

As I got older, I became aware of the strength she possessed and the tragedies she endured, including those with my own grandmother. Looking at her, you could never guess what she had survived. I have searched my mind, but can never remember seeing her cry. When she died, an era in our family was gone. There were not many reasons to go back to that tiny town. Nothing was quite the same.

Occasionally, I look back to those days as some of the best of life. She left a legacy of integrity, strength, commitment, and hard work, along with a love of baking, and unwavering faith and trust in God. After her death, my grandmother was never quite the same. She eventually moved in with my parents. Back then I did not realize what was happening, but in hindsight, I knew something was terribly wrong. Something harsh and cruel seemed to occur in her inner being.

Although away in college, I lived home during breaks. Having access to her was wonderful. I could always expect down home cooking that only a grandmother could provide. And, believe me, my Mom is a fabulous cook. I had heard stories of her breakdowns as a child but had never personally experienced them. I would often witness strange behavior but she always seemed fine when interrupted. I assumed her episodes were a part of "her normal character." I enjoyed conversations and gained wisdom and knowledge at her feet that would be used over my lifetime. She encouraged me in ways few could. Her words were always soothing.

She saw the best in me. I envisioned the children I had yet to bear enjoying what was perhaps one of the most unique relationships ever, between a great-grand parent and a child. The thought of knowing someone your grandmother at some point had to listen to was a wonder. Yes, my children would someday have a great-grandmother. The thought was thrilling, one I was certain they would enjoy as I had until at least their late teens or twenties. They would gain nuggets of wisdom, knowledge, and experience only one with gray hair, in the fourth generation had. The experience would give them an edge many could never comprehend.

My grandmother had uncanny ways. For instance, *whatever* she said about *anything* would happened and generally exactly as she said. Also, they would happen shortly after she mentioned them. When her counsel was heeded it saved hard-learned lessons. Advice one would rather not hear from parents came easy from her. Little problems back then would dissipate after a few moments of conversation.

At times she would caution me to be careful of certain people who would ultimately "show their colors." She was the first to tell me a young man I was dating was in love with me, although I had no inkling, and neither did he. She was the first to tell me I was pregnant almost from the moment of conception. How did she know things and why was she so accurate?

She could not understand why she needed a new dress for my wedding when she already had several she considered okay. She questioned spending on a wedding she felt could be simpler and admonished me to focus more on the marriage. Her advice was to love each other; keep your family out of your business; don't take a fight between you and your husband to your family; and, never take advice about your marriage from anyone who had not been married at least as long as you have.

She advised me to be careful of those who had been divorced because there was "something" they did not get right, and, to never take marital advice from a single person. Her view on that topic alone is a book. She would jokingly say to even screen her on the topic. She said there would be good times and bad times but as long as at least one person is willing to fight for the marriage, it would last. "Just so you don't give up at the same time. That is when a marriage is over."

She said you only get one shot at life, so make the most of it. She said that people hinder progress. She believed dreams were meant to be lived and chances taken—the bigger, the better. She also said that those who ridiculed a dream probably didn't have one worth mentioning. "No matter how big a dream, it ain't bigger than God's mind." Dreams test your limits and show what you are made of. She said trials make or break a person, and when you see a broken man or woman, you see broken dreams.

People with dreams get up even when they fall down because they have something to live for. She believed experience to be the best teacher. She knew I had book sense, because I had always been an honors student, but warned me to make sure to have some common sense too. She said that in the real world it would get you further than any book could.

She said to be respected was the best thing, because no matter what you do, everyone will not love you, because some people don't love themselves. She admonished that "pretty is as pretty does." And, that the prettiest person in the world is ugly if they do not treat others kind. She said to never wear your problems on your sleeves. When you are at your worst that is when you should look your best. Of course she mentioned the basics, do unto others, be kind, don't be afraid to give. Good always comes back. Pick up after yourself, look people in the eyes, and love everybody, no matter how they treat you. She said the mean ones need love the most.

Kindness is a gift you give to yourself. Every kind act is rewarded, if not with you, with your children or some other family member in need. And no matter where you go or what you do, always acknowledge and respect your elders.

She said anything you become accustomed to paying others to do, be sure you learn to do yourself. She also had funny ones like don't leave hair in your comb or let anyone use it. She said, "When she dies, she would have no regrets, because she lived her way." I had no reason to believe my children would not enjoy the privilege of a great-grandmother; but, shortly after my grandmother moved in with my parents problems surfaced.

Shattered Pieces

I transferred to a local University because I wanted a new car and it made economic sense. During those last two years of school, I lived at home with my parents and my dear grandmother. My great-grandmother was deceased a short time when her emotional problems surfaced. She experienced a nervous breakdown that produced subhuman strength, manic highs, paranoia, and irrational behavior. In hindsight I had always noticed things, but overlooked them as a part of her quirky, eccentric, behavior. At times, the emotional turmoil was unbearable for my mother, but she was unwavering in devotion.

For some reason, when my grandmother had episodes, I was the only one she seemed to recognize who could soothe the savage beast within. Not once did she lash out or attempt to harm me as she did others. Still, her vague stare told me she was barely, there, if there at all. She would destroy portions of the house by pulling down blinds, tearing, throwing, and breaking things. When I walked in, she calmed down. In the midst of her rages, there was always a humane place to discuss life as if nothing was wrong. But, the distant, glazed look reminded everyone of her illness. It was determined to rob her of her sanity. My heart ached for my mother who seemed helpless. My father did not know what to do.

That was the beginning of several hospital bouts. The doctors thought many things, but especially the death of her mother somehow triggered the episodes. Not dealing with the death, surfaced in the form of extreme manic behavior. She was given medication that made her sluggish, indifferent, and distant. At one point, she rationalized that if she took all of it, she would no longer feel lethargic. That decision almost cost her life.

Classes were over for the day. I came home to change for my part-time job. During the day, both my parents worked, so my grandmother was home alone. Because of her age she rarely climbed the stairs. Her room was downstairs, so her being upstairs was unusual. I came home, always happy to see her no matter what her state of mind. I looked into her room. She was nowhere to be found. Not even in the kitchen where she could easily be located. As I climbed the stairs, I had the eeriest feeling. Completing the journey validated my suspicions. She lay near my bedroom, eyes rolled back, with a faint snore. I phoned my mother at work and called 911.

I called my mother back to give her the name of the hospital where she would be taken. Within minutes, the ambulance arrived. The paramedics were pumping, injecting, and working on her. I was horrified! The entire scene was a nightmare, except I was wide-awake. "Oh, please God don't let her die and certainly not this way."

The paramedics loaded her on the back of the ambulance, which took a while because she was a big woman. They struggled, huffing and puffing as they discussed the best way to get her downstairs, through the door, and ultimately into the ambulance. That scene actually broke the shock and provided a brief moment of humor 'til this day. I rode in back with her. By the time the ambulance arrived, my mother was at the hospital. They worked on her for quite sometime. Thank God they saved her.

Mental illness is one of the cruelest tricks of life. The stigma and the shame can prevent those who need help most from seeking it; yet, it is common in many families, in many forms. Once exposed, everyone bears its ugly scars. The one time we discussed the incident, she informed me that she in no way intended to die, but to stop the pain. She hated the way the medicine made her feel.

She felt great remorse for putting her family and herself through the turmoil. But, rationalized that if she took everything at one time, that would be it, and she could get on with life. Her mind, like others with mental disorders played a cruel trick that almost cost her life. That was the last time any major emotional problems surfaced. As a matter of fact, after that the remainder of her emotional life was fairly calm with the exception of a few nervous moments that she always seemed to control. Perhaps the thought of the experience prevented her from going there again.

One of the hallmarks of our relationship was discussing everything. We talked about the incident once and never again, not because I did not want to, but because I was fearful that bringing it up would somehow trigger another episode. Everyone was aware of what happened, but there was a knowing, an unspoken code to never "speak it" again. Time passed, things got back to normal.

I planned a wedding, moved, and prepared for life in a different city. Still, living in the same state afforded frequent visits home. The saying remains true—there is no place like home! When I had my first child, the one she spoke of, my grandmother and my parents were eagerly waiting to see her. My grandmother adored her great-granddaughter and delighted in her presence. She would take over and attend to her every need, commenting on how beautiful and smart she was and that someday she would do something great.

My daughter was her second great-grandchild, who along with her great-nieces brought joy to her soul. Eventually, we moved to another state. Once we moved, I could only come home once or twice a year. On one of those visits as I sat in her room, I noticed when she moved; she seemed to be in excruciating pain. I asked my mother about it. She confirmed my suspicions. She said that she would not go to the doctor as she had suggested. I told her I would get her to go.

We talked and eventually discussed her pain. She admitted it was great and she was also bleeding. I asked her why not go to a doctor, but knew the answer. She feared them. Many seniors who live most of their lives without doctors, figure, what's the point? I convinced her to go and promised to go with her. She agreed.

When the doctor called her into the examination room, her eyes spoke to mine, as a child would, "You are coming aren't you?" The doctor and nurse proceeded towards the examination room, both looking as if to say, "You are not going in, are you?" I said, "I'm going in," our silent agreement. She nodded.

She was afraid, but the examination was crucial. I could tell from their expressions something was wrong. Something was very wrong. She flinched throughout the examination. The doctor said test results would be ready in a few days. I took her home and told my mother what the doctor said. I assured my grandmother that no matter what if she had to return, I would come back and go with her.

"Last Call"

The telephone rang. My mother was on the other end. "Your grandmother is ill." Over a period of months my grandmother was in and out of the hospital. She lost over one hundred pounds of her almost three hundred pound frame. Eventually her bedroom was turned into a mini-hospital ward. Much of that time I lived over two thousand miles away and could not be there as often as I liked. During her final days, my mother assisted by my aunt attended to her every need. I spoke with her almost everyday. At times she could barely speak. Other times she was her old self.

My mother wrote a letter about her illness, that it was taking her life. I was livid! How dare she say that? In hindsight, how brave and difficult that must have been. She put her feelings aside to prepare the grandchildren who adored her for her departure. I flew in to visit her at the hospital. I told her I would return in a couple of months around Mother's Day, and that I had found her a wonderful gift.

My grandmother told me to be sure to bring my daughter on my next visit. She told me not to worry about a gift because she would not need anything. In her way, she was telling me she was dying, but I rejected the message. There was no doubt in her mind or in that of her only child.

I returned for that final visit with my daughter. At one point, she was fixated on something staring, entranced, but peaceful. I had to return home, but spoke with her daily during that final week. Most times, her voice was barely audible. On the last evening, I asked if she was leaving. Weakly, she mustered "uh huh." I begged her not to go, but all she said was "uh huh" as if she had to heed the call awaiting her. Her earthly body had enough. She accepted her fate.

When the telephone rang early the next morning, I knew it was the worse news imaginable. "Your grandmother is gone." I lost it, but in hindsight should have focused on my mother's feelings, her only child. She cared for and watched her suffer daily. She had suffered the greater loss. I was on the first available flight home that day. My daughter was only three years old. It never dawned on me that she would not experience the love of a great-grandmother. I felt cheated. The family had a history of long life, but she did not make her three and ten as she desired. Everyone seemed to make it to at least seventy, well past it. Why the shift and why now?

She was buried in that small east Texas town in a family plot. Everyone was numb. I went on a four-year journey before accepting her death. I had lost other relatives, including my great-grandmother, but my grandmother's death was the first that affected my very soul. A piece of me died that day. No one would ever think of me the way she did. No one would ever accept every flaw and still love me unconditionally.

I could not discuss the pain with my mother because as strong a face as she presented, I knew she was grieved beyond measure. My sister and I would discuss it on occasion, but the loss was just too painful. I found myself thousands of miles away with a husband who could not understand my grief, not because he did not try, but because the pain was too great. Somehow, I had to find my own way. I was in the sieve. Over time, God used her death to nurture a faith that would be tried but would remain strong.

Mirror Image

I went on a spiritual journey like none other. I went back to college hoping to find new meaning in life. I took religious courses and read life books to fill the void. I dreamed of my grandmother often and eventually met a lovely older, grandmotherly type. We became dear friends. She was from a distant country, worldly, and well traveled. Her presence was illuminating. She was stunning. I was exposed to and learned things by association that most could only imagine and few would believe.

She began to share things, out of the blue, familiar, things. At some point, I found out that she did tea leaves readings. She read for a very distinct and elite group of personalities. There was an endless list of those who would not make decisions without her input. As a result of her lifestyle, I experienced some amazing things and meet a plethora of interesting people. Opportunities that most in a lifetime could only imagine, let alone have privy to, I enjoyed regularly. Eventually, as a favor, she offered to read for me.

Her accuracy was uncanny, no other way to describe it! Like my grandmother, she knew things she had no way of knowing. Things I had only discussed with few people, if any, but had never shared with her. For the first time since my grandmother's death, I found peace in a strange, uneasy way. Although I attempted to get additional readings, for some reason they never happened. No matter how well planned, something would always come up to prevent them.

I spent a great deal of time with my friend shopping, dining, sailing, looking at rare jewels, art, fabrics, and browsing antique stores. We often ate meals she prepared. She was also a magnificent cook, but with a flair for the exotic. She exposed me to foods from other worlds. Many I still love to this day. She had a particular art for selecting wines and we often visited local vineyards.

I spent a great deal of time at her upscale home receiving nuggets of wisdom. She always amazed me. I was addicted to her presence. Often and out of the blue, she would share specific intimate details about family members she had never met, personal things, quirky habits, and tidbits. When my husband would stop by the job with my daughter, she would suggest I bring her over, but something would always happen to prevent their meeting. Now I know that was the Holy Spirit protecting her pure spirit.

Throughout our friendship, she never once visited my home and I never invited her. I did not realize that until years later and still find that strange. Deep down I knew something was not quite right, but ignored that inner voice. A close friend and confidant warned me to be careful. She thought that something was strange about her. She admitted that she seemed great and was even impressed with her accuracy, but unlike my other friends who visited; who could not wait to see her, she was not anxious to meet her. She reminded me of how naturally suspicious I was of most things and people.

Looking back, strange things happened during that time. I had two close encounters with death. One, a brown recluse spider bite that even the doctors professed was a miracle that I survived. The other was a severe case of pneumonia. I was hospitalized for more three weeks. In addition, I suffered some "weird" ailments, happenings, and strange dreams. Prior to that time, I had never been ill, not even with a cold. And, certainly had no major health related issues.

Since then, I confessed, repented, and asked God to break any strongholds, iniquities, or attachments that season may have caused I renounced all familiar spirits against me, and my bloodline. On one of my drives to her house, I noticed a particular church on the way.

Since my move from the south, I never neglected attending, although it was more of a habit than anything else. Now all of a sudden, I felt something about my new find. As large as the "new church" was, I had never paid any attention to it. It was a few miles from my friend's house. For some reason, I had to attend. I discussed it with my husband, even though I never discussed those readings until later in life and began going to a church led by an incredible Pastor. Although I never officially joined, I attended faithfully for over three years until moving to another part of the state.

His messages fueled my soul. They gave me zeal and clarity, but most of all peace that had eluded me since my grandmother's passing. I began to read his books and any others he mentioned during his sermons. Under him, I learned to study The Word and apply it to my life. The more I attended, the more peaceful I became, and the less I saw of my friend. His sound doctrine along with his love of the Lord caused me to refocus and question everything that was not of God. God used him to reveal truth, restore my soul, keep me from evil, but most of all to get me back on a sound spiritual path.

His messages were simple. He used sound biblical teachings that any person could appreciate—saved or not. He questioned any and everything that was not of God. Though deep and profound, he presented in a manner that would not alienate the newest convert. Each Sunday sitting near that front section, I felt empowered.

After I had attended for about seven months, the Pastor did a sermon on "familiar spirits." How the enemy uses them to lure, attract, disguise and destroy lives. Apparently, my spirit was prepared because as soon as he began to speak, a light bulb went off. I was convicted immediately. I had been spiritually vulnerable. My association with my friend gave the enemy a legal foothold to operate in certain areas of my life. Furthermore, because of the void from my grandmother, I was easy prey for a grandmotherly type, my specific need and weakness at that time.

Had it not been for God's covering, that lack of knowledge could have destroyed me. Thankfully, God protects his children in ignorance. That is grace and great news! Once I received that revelation, I never saw her again. Oh, I spoke with her over the telephone several times, even made plans to connect and travel abroad with her, but through a series of events lost complete contact.

As suddenly as she appeared, she was gone. I was sad because I really loved and adored her. How could I have been so gullible? Over time, I came to understand how the enemy uses any method to bind you. He makes evil and sin attractive, wraps it in a beautiful, tailored made package, and presents it with "a big ole bow" and a smile. He appears as light, but be aware. Learn to test the spirits. She was a wonderful person, but did things and believed things that were contrary to His word and my core beliefs. Had I applied The Word, that relationship would have ended as quickly as it began.

The Holy Spirit always guides you with truth. He protects you, but you must pay attention. Since then I have never looked back and often thank God for using that season to bring me completely back to Him. Knowledge is power and the enemy is crafty, providing exactly what is needed. Without a doubt, God led me through the pain of that season, protected me and kept me from danger. That season was my first in the sieve.

I went on with life, had another child, the son my friend said I would have. We relocated, coming full circle, back to our roots in the town where I was most comfortable. Because of our entrepreneurial spirits, my husband and I tried several business ventures, hitting and missing until we found several that worked. During that time, additional cash was needed to sustain the business and provide basic needs. I took a job at a high profiled church as an Administrative Assistant. The pay was terrible and in my opinion a huge step backwards from the positions I had since college, the previous one with a tenured politician.

Working in the political arena was one of the most challenging jobs ever—physically, emotionally, and spiritually, but that position gave me a platform to coordinate and oversee major events. More importantly, it gave me a forum to get paid for writing. Virtually everything required some sort of proposal, agenda, plan, brochure, press kit, or the like. I experienced and interacted with people who made major decisions, one became President.

Although I loved the fast, unpredictable pace and was intrigued with the political world, I knew that staying in that arena would ultimately break my soul and keep me from my family. Self-aggrandizement was the norm and cutting throats were certainly not the exception. Everyone was there promoting their agendas, no matter what.

My politician was one of the most tenured in the "House." He was not perfect, but he was a perfectionist. Nothing was ever right and everything had to be done over, at least once. Like most high-powered individuals, he was accustomed to being catered to, and most gladly accommodated him. His demanding nature forced me to bring my best game to the workforce and taught me a unique lesson in survival.

Workdays consisted of reviewing and monitoring legislation; coordinating committee and caucus meetings, planning events, and reviewing and documenting everything. In addition, we dealt with media, constituents and lobbyists. We spent a great deal of the day attending to their needs. Those hours on the house floor were grueling but gave me the opportunity to learn first hand how the world worked. While there, I heard some of the greatest speakers of our time.

Watching a bill become a law or the passion of those who really fight for our rights is an art form. My politician's inability to be pleased actually fuelled my desire for excellence. For some reason, he seemed to like me. He did not rage as he did with the others. Unlike many staff members, I did not mind or complain about getting his tea with the appropriate amount of sugar, or having the paper on his desk with articles about him clipped for review. I certainly did not talk about him behind his back, no matter what he did. Those extra things did not diminish me and unlike others I refused to complain. Most things I considered time savers that would allow for other more important things and get him out of the office quicker into the House Chambers.

Besides, human compassion knows no boundaries and I did my work as unto the Lord. Some tried to make more out of it than it was, but that too is a part of that arena. Naturally good people do all kinds of things to promote themselves, including sabotage. Over time, I learned to ignore many of the biting stings and came to understand that most who faithfully serve considered it a calling to affect positive change.

Somehow I knew my skin was not thick enough to remain, but admire those who heed the call to serve their Constituents. That politician has been a great resource and has often provided referrals for other business. I look back over that period and still cannot imagine how I got through it, but it was a springboard to bigger and better things. God used that forum to develop new levels of commitment, professionalism and determination. Working in politics taught me that if I could survive there, I could survive.

"It's A Set Up"

Working for a church would be quite the transition, I thought. It was one of the largest in the city, led by a leader with a reputation for excellence. I knew many who would work in any capacity just for the affiliation. One good word from him could open doors that may otherwise remain shut. At first, taking the job was strictly a cash move. We needed money. Every decision was critical in obtaining that goal.

Once hired, I found that the position was not actually with the church, but the non-profit arm of the organization. Several weeks passed before I pursued it. My husband and I prayed. Actually he insinuated I would be crazy not to take it considering our financial state. I went to the interview and met with the Executive Director, *a nice older lady*. It went well.

Before I left she requested that I write a paragraph on why she should hire me. I thought, it is only an administrative assistant. That statement certainly does not discount their roles. Most are the backbones of great organizations. They are the leaders behind the leaders, often, knowing as much if not more than the leaders they report to. They are invaluable. Good ones are certainly the backbone of any organization.

> *What are often considered Setbacks are "Setups" by God.*

They wield power within the organization. I admire those with the gift. It is certainly a gift to find a great one. Being in that position taught me the value of "the little things" that are the huge difference. Some of the greatest leaders have the best assistants. Over the years as I have grown my own business, that position which requires excellence, trust, skills, and most of all loyalty is sometimes the hardest to fill. Anyhow, I wrote the piece, thanked her, and left not really caring whether or not she would call, but had a sense of peace about the whole thing.

Not only did the Executive Director call, she offered me the job. She was very excited. I considered it a step backwards and thought it would not be challenging. I did not want to be confined to an office all day. Nevertheless,

I began my job with the attitude that I have with most things--if I am going to do it, it will be done well. I believe in an "extra mile mentality." I worked as unto the Lord and relied on Him to bless my efforts.

I had no idea that the Executive Director had only been there a few months. She relocated because of health matters and went back into the work force to specifically take that job. She was a proficient and highly skilled Administrator who knew how to get projects funded. She came to rely heavily upon me. Whatever she gave me, I did, one shot, one time with minimal effort. That developed a level of trust and confidence where she involved me in literally everything.

Under the helm of the Executive Director, programs and services grew by leaps and bounds. Eventually I functioned in several positions within the organization, including, Community Outreach, Fundraising, Events Coordinator, and Editor of the monthly newsletter with my own monthly column. I assisted with developing policy and procedural manuals, personnel guides, and more importantly grants management and development. The Executive Director became more than a boss. She became a professional mentor and a friend.

She was an older, grandmotherly type but her familiar spirit was one that I had known all of my life. She had the presence of God and knew His power. She was also the daughter of a well-known minister from the Civil Rights era. We prayed together, which is unheard of in most work environments. She allowed me to travel on behalf of the organization, attend conferences and meet with officials. Many of whom I had crossed paths with in my previous job.

She recognized and acknowledged three very strong gifts I possessed—technical writing, planning, and program development. Since they were things I naturally loved, I did not consider them special. I had always done them in some capacity, from a very young age. She allowed me to operate the central office, which included overseeing at least seven grant funded projects. I was consistently exposed to many high profiled individuals, including direct access to the Chairman of the Board, who was the senior Pastor.

I loved the way he conducted business. To this day, I utilize a specific technique I observed whenever I met with him or observed him conduct meetings. He taught me to be 100% prepared. If you went before him unprepared, you missed an opportunity. He was tough, but always seemed pleased with my efforts. His intensity intimidated most, but it was obvious to me that he was a great guy. What are often considered setbacks are actually setups by God positioning you for bigger, better, things. Faithfulness in small things increase your capacity to obtain bigger ones.

I began to write almost daily. When I worked on grants and proposals, time would literally fly. Unlike the rest of the staff who dreaded the task, I looked forward to writing deadlines, regardless of their nature or complexity. Still, in the midst of it, my entrepreneurial nature could not be quenched. While there, I continued side projects. Eventually, I began a part time project with the School District. Since the Executive Director and I were totally transparent, she encouraged me to pursue personal ventures as long as they did not hinder my work.

She was unaware that I am more productive when operating in overloaded. I had a private office, which made it easy to juggle outside projects. Eventually, they began to compete with work. Because I felt called to assist in developing the infrastructure of the organization I stayed. Almost every grant that was submitted was funded and a donor base to be reckoned with was established. Of course being affiliated with a mega church was certainly a bonus.

Even though I had more flexibility than I would have had on any other job and loved the security of the agency, I began to feel weighted with the routine. After discussing it with my husband, I made the decision to leave the organization to develop my own business. Now, I am certain a position I was reluctant to take, refined my skills and gave me spunk to pursue my life's work.

Had I rejected it, I would have missed the place God wanted me during that season and the lessons needed for new levels. I definitely would not have the proficiency as a grant writer or fund developer were it not for that organization. I am eternally grateful for everyone there but I am just a natural born entrepreneur. Entrepreneurs have a drive to pursue, create, and conquer and are willing to risk everything for a chance at fulfilling their dream.

The entertainment industry is a great example of the entrepreneurial spirit. Those who make it big know there is no such thing as "an overnight sensation." No matter how hard to conform to the norm their chance at the exception is more challenging and rewarding. Many forgo comforts that most would never consider doing without for the chance to make their mark on the world. Most never have to wonder what if, because most have pursued their passion. These are not the seniors sitting around wondering and wishing what they could or should have done. Yet, those who cannot endure harsh scrutiny, alienation, rejection, gossip, discomfort, and extreme sacrifice should never consider entrepreneurship.

Risks can cause you to become an outcast. Risks takers make the world exciting. I surround myself with big vision people who force my thinking out of the box. I limit time with narrow thinking, negative individuals. Negative, critical, judgmental people generally have limited or low vision. They will hinder you because they can never see or risk beyond what "they see." Without risk things remain mundane. Risk push the world forward. Be assured that people like Bill Gates pay a hefty price for their big visions, but I am sure all of his nay Sayers are still wondering what happened. When risks pay off, it pays big. When it does not, life can be miserable, but it is worth it for a chance at something amazing.

Life should be lived, the bigger the risk, the greater the reward, the more faith needed. The key to achieving purpose is being in the right place at the right time. And, it really does not matter how you start, but that you finish and finish well. Blessings do not always come in the form you want, but in the form you need.

What I know for sure is there are many sifted seasons, some harsher than others. All are designed to create permanent change. God use them to refocus, recreate, perfect, and refine things needed for new levels. Brokenness is often the path to insight, inspiration, tolerance, patience, and ultimately success. Doors that close, people who are removed during those periods are no longer meant to be there. When the final change happens, new doors new people, and new opportunities will guide you to your destiny.

The purpose is clear to understand that there is no help except God. You will know the difference between sifting by God and by the enemy. The enemy rocks your world to the core with challenges, tragedies and adversities in hopes that you fail. He dedicates a special group of demons to assure no relief. He desires to destroy you and does not stop until you surrender. He gnaws until there is nothing left, attacking areas you cannot overlook, like your health, family, finances, relationships, and basic security.

When you are sifted, mountains stand strong. As you overcome one, another awaits. Paraphrasing my previous Pastor, "The enemy has an old fashioned whuppin stick and wants to wear your behind out." Sifting obviously involves some sort of spiritual laws beyond human comprehension. The story of Job clearly exemplifies that certain areas are negotiated prior to sifting. Others remain off limits.

Over time, some things become clearer. Like Job, your sifting may include everything but death, but like him "you shall come forth as pure gold." Once the ordained lessons are learned, the suddenlies suddenly ends. You will bear the scars of the season. My first time left both emotional and physical scars.

Shattered Parts

…Fast forward to winter on an early Saturday morning. A morning that as a wife and mother is precious and rare-- home alone. My family decided to take a three-hour drive to visit my mother-in-law for the day. The moment they left, my spirit was uneasy. I said to myself, "They do not need to go today." I stayed behind to relax and make an afternoon appointment. Since I was up, I made phone calls to confirm the meeting and time instead of beginning the day in prayer.

Over the approximate seventeen years since I began daily devotion, I have remained faithful, and cannot recall deviating from the routine. Putting God at the beginning of the day is a privilege I look forward to each morning. Even when I travel, I always spend time alone with Him, first. There I receive insight and wisdom to handle whatever is before me. That time is the most precious, non-negotiable part of my every day. God confirms or redirects my agenda during that quiet time. He often shows me things I need to know, and yes even warns me of things to come. It is the only uninterrupted time I have during the day.

Things were out of sync because everyone was rushing to leave. Once they were on their way I began devotion, but remained restless, alarmed, vexed. About five minutes into prayer the telephone rang. I assumed it was one of my family members, especially my young son who loved to call from the cellular phone. When I answered, I heard the most horrific sound ever from the mouth of my teenaged daughter. She was talking through hysterical screams and apparently hyperventilating. I did not know what had happened, but I knew it was awful.

I could hear my son crying in the background. Somehow I convinced my daughter to calm down long enough to tell me there had been a terrible accident, a three-car collision a few miles from their destination. Their father would not wake up. I asked who was there and she said a man appeared from behind a tree with a walkie-talkie who told them to get out of the smoking car. He informed them that he called 911, and emergency vehicles were on the way.

I asked to speak with him, but my daughter said he was no longer there, but a fireman was working on their dad. I heard major chaos in the background. I told my daughter, she would have to attend to her brother. I heard sirens full blast. I told my daughter to let them do their jobs. They would take care of daddy. I could also hear noise in the background that sounded like an airplane. The Paramedic said they were life-flighting my husband to a Critical Care Unit in a nearby city, the same city that would have been their destination.

I knew something awful had happened that would affect everything for a very long time. Both children suffered injuries and remained in the hospital most of the day. Their father did not fare so well. He was in the battle of his life. I made a couple of calls, letting key people know what had happened. For some reason everyone was unavailable. I finally got in touch with my sister. I knew she would stand in my stead until I arrived.

Both children would be comfortable with her there. I was somewhat relieved to know she would be there too. Since it would take some time to arrive, I informed my daughter that her Aunt was in route. That seemed to provide some comfort. I discussed specifics to the best of my capabilities. I implored that she arrive by the time the children did and told her that I would leave shortly.

There was a terrible rainstorm that day. A drive that would normally take no longer than three-hours turned into the longest of my life. God blessed our family with the gift to operate effectively in crisis. We rarely react during a crisis, but in our own time, most often when alone. Once I made calls, I waited for instructions from the medical team.

The children were transported in different ambulances. I was especially concerned about my youngest being without someone for even a moment. The paramedics assured me they would be fine and would arrive together. One would be taken to the Pediatrics the other to Emergency. I told my sister to go to Pediatrics. I told my daughter her Aunt would go there first.

I prayed for strength and guidance. I asked God to give me grace for whatever was before me and mercy for my family. In that moment I instinctively asked for my husband's life. God spoke in my spirit, "He would live, not die." I knew that no matter what, he would live. I gathered some things for my journey--clothes, insurance papers, check books, my Bible, journal, and a few family photos.

> *I did not know what had happened, but I knew it was aweful!*

My mind filled with whys because we had been in a difficult season. It seemed like it was over. I was certain we had entered a season of rest and restoration. It had been approximately a year since we restructured. During our difficulties help could barely be found. Like most, our season exposed our true support system. I thought about another one prior to that one when my husband's son moved in. Before moving in at seventeen, no one except his father had ever laid eyes on him or his family. Throughout his life, there was very little contact, though his father made numerous attempts.

Along with his quiet, gentle, spirit and incredible artistic talent, were some other complicated things. Many grieved my spirit, but he was now a part of our family and family dealt with things together. Overall, he was a wonderful "kid." He was an amazing artist. God seemed to reveal things that I would question. Amazingly, he would answer honestly. Fortunately, he opened up and discussed things from his past, perhaps for the very first time. Since he is naturally quiet, that alone was a miracle. Overall and over time, he did well under our roof, but when the time came for him to be on his own, he had challenges.

There was always something but he was grown and had to experience life as an adult. Like many children, he was a good kid who experienced some bad things. Eventually, he moved back home, and is now a very productive young man, but more importantly a great servant for the Lord. I wondered why things could not be normal. I drove to the hospital while thinking about scenarios like these. This time about my younger son who also experienced his share of problems. I learned some things about adults who envy and judge through an innocent child. I learned that many things are still very prevalent today.

My son's new school was a problem. They tried to kill his spirit, label him. Many schools are businesses often used as fronts for narrow minded, limited skilled, underexposed individuals to perpetrate misnomers on the very children who need them most. Those who do not conform to their clique or club mentality are prime targets. They are methodical in exclusion to assure that they remained positioned for funding and exemplary status and will quickly discard any flaws to their systems. Without intervention, ignorance could alter a child's esteem and wreak undue havoc for years.

Since they are rarely held accountable, parents must be aware and know their children's capabilities. Otherwise, they could fall prey to the hidden traps within the very system that should protect them. We did not accept an opinion that was contrary to what we knew was truth. He was brilliant and we challenged an entire system on his behalf. Thoughts raced because it appeared a new season had emerged.

Recently, my husband closed two substantial business deals and my Consulting business was steady. Our daughter was in her last year of high school at a performing arts school and was selected to participate in the city's Voice Opera Studio, a major feat for a young vocalist. She began auditioning at various colleges throughout the country. My son was doing great in school, met some wonderful friends, and made honor roll. Everything was coming together, the breakthrough was on hand and life seemed normal. But, that call changed everything.

The previous seasons were minor compared to the one before us now. Somehow, God must have known a pre sifting would be necessary to endure the unthinkable. In all of my years of living, this would become the worse experience of my entire life. To this day, I still have not fully comprehended it. I thought about it, but did not allow myself to question God. I knew He was Sovereign even in this.

I wanted to plead for the family, to remind him of how hard things had been, to let him know that no matter how little we had, we never wavered on tithing and in many cases sacrificial offerings; to tell him that the children entrusted to us were being trained in His ways. They loved and obeyed Him. They were great, children that anyone would be proud of. Lord, can't you see? Lord, don't you know how weary, so why now? Why can't we just have a regular season like everyone else? But, I knew man could not bargain with God.

I decided to go alone. In crisis, I have to be alone, to think, to be, and pray. I cannot stand chatter or talk when facing crisis or making major decisions. I prefer total silence, which can make others uncomfortable. Anything other than that is unbearable. Both my Mom and best friend pleaded for me to wait, but I went alone.

It "rained cats and dogs" the entire time. I could only go about 45 miles per hour. I thought nothing could happen to me because the children would not be able to handle it, so I was extremely careful, driving slower to assure a safe arrival. This turned my three-hour drive into more than fours. Every fifteen minutes or so, I would receive calls from my ten-year old. "Mom, are you here yet?" Both children were eager to see their father, but I informed family members they could not until I arrived. I called my brother-in-law whose walk I've always admired.

He performed our marriage ceremony and has profound insight into the things of God. He and his wife are prayer warriors and Anointed Prophets. I knew that as soon as I called they would begin interceding. It was not unusual for me to call, so when he picked up the telephone he said, "Hi, how is it going?" Except this time it was not going well. I told him about the accident; and, that his brother had been life-flighted to a hospital. I informed him that I was on the way there; and, that I was calling for prayer.

He took a few moments to get over the shock, but quickly regrouped and began to pray over my travels, the children, and especially his brother's life. He affirmed that my husband would live. They organized a prayer vigil. The next few hours were a series of telephone calls from the hospital about the care of my entire family.

Living Dead

My husband was in a critical care unit. I was being asked to give permission via telephone for a procedure to be done to eliminate fluid on his brain. Doctors had to insert a tube by making an incision in his head to drain the fluid from his brain. The entire thing was like watching a horror movie, except we were in it. The hospital called several times about the children's care. By the time I arrived, many family members were there. I was particularly concerned about his Mother who had already lost a child. I sensed her fear and could only imagine the thought of her possibly losing another.

The Neurosurgeon informed me that my husband suffered severe head trauma and was in a coma. The actual medical term used was Subarachnoid Hemorrhage, he was in a coma. He said that the next 48 hours would be critical. He informed me the he might wake up fine; he might never come out of the coma; he might wake up and not know anyone; he might wake up and be a vegetable; or, he might not wake up at all. He allowed me to ask questions. He was a man of science but I knew that he was also a believer.

Although the doctor warned me, nothing could prepare me for what I would see. There were tubes coming from every direction. I opened his eyes, looked inside, but there was no life. I began a soft cry and a prayer. I prayed in his ear and I prayed to God. I asked God to let him live because in that moment I forgot the promise He made before leaving home--that he would live and not die. I spoke into his ear believing he could somehow hear. I told him we had gone through too much for him to die now. The children needed him. Ours was not a perfect marriage, but we had been at it for almost twenty years and that bond sustained us.

ICU allows two people per visit for brief periods. I went in alone during my second visit to see, absorb, and pray. I knew the power of God was on display. My actions and emotions would set the tone of that entire emergency room. Friends, family, and especially the children would follow my lead and attempt to believe as I did, no matter how difficult. I was acutely aware of the various faith levels or not. I knew there were those who did not know God as healer, miracle worker, or deliverer.

This was a concern; since I believe great faith yields great results. I even knew that many feared the inevitable, but that did not matter. I was acutely aware of those who mocked me and my faith, but did not care. This was bigger than human stuff. If God did not move, my husband would die. "If I was going to be a fool, I would do it believing God." Somehow, I knew God had a plan, though no clue of the specifics. Everyone involved had arrived at destiny to a divine appointment. All would receive lessons tailored made for them.

God arranged it so that everyone who needed to be available was there. As my husband often said, "The situation was non-negotiable." There were two choices, life or death. The latter was out. I was not willing to enter into contracts with anyone except the Lord, my Savior. I had no doubt that God could raise, heal and deliver at anytime. He had power over death and if it was not his will for him to die, he would live. In that moment, I made a choice to trust God. Unwavering belief was the only hope. Besides, from the looks of things, there was nothing else.

Fear and doubt was a major concern because faith and fear are ineffective in the same space. The greater one cancels the other and wins. In the natural, even I knew the situation appeared hopeless, but knew beyond a shadow of a doubt that I served one who specialized in impossibilities. Although I doubted many things, I never doubted God! Paraphrasing Daniel when trapped in the lions den, I emphatically said, "I serve the God who delivers, but even if He does not, He is still God." The same God who raised Lazarus from death would raise my husband. God had everyone's attention.

At the time of the accident, I was participating in a group study on faith. Since I often train after hours, I informed clients, family, and friends that I was unavailable Tuesday evenings until I finished. The accident occurred during the ninth session. As always the facilitator was awesome. I was excited about things stirring in my spirit. I remember the facilitator saying that each time God increase your faith, there will be a faith test. We were given a blue string to wear around our wrist as a reminder of our covenant and at the end of the study presented bookmarks with faith professions. Each time I walked to or from ICU, her words resonated in my spirit. I repeated them going and coming.

Imagining the voices of those women infused me to stay strong. I envisioned the facilitator on that platform admonishing me to believe. I could sense her saying "Girlfriend, now this is the faith test I warned you about." To this day I still have that marker with the blue card attached in my Bible. The facilitator said no matter what she went through, she would trust God for the outcome. I envisioned her in that crowded church not knowing me from "Eve" saying, "If you perish girlfriend, you better perish believing God."

That study prepared me for the faith test of a lifetime. I felt that God had somehow prepared me for sifting, but this was the ultimate shakedown. I said, "God this is too big for me, I have no control, but it is nothing for you. Here is your son. His life is in your hands." I believed like never before. There was a life at stake and someone had to believe. I thought if it were me, in the same situation, I would want someone who believed as if they were lying on that bed themselves. I pray for that leader and her ministry often.

Additionally, I was facilitating a growth group at my own church. In spite of the drive, I continued teaching it, driving the two and a half hours to fulfill my obligation. I informed the group of the situation and assured them I would do everything to complete the classes. They seemed shocked that I was willing. I told them to follow my example and let nothing prevent them from obtaining their breakthrough. They all remained faithful.

God was doing something. He would use the situation to heal relationships and restore others. Anyone who ever questioned Him was about to experience Him firsthand. Something greater than medical science was at work. Even though I was certain that my husband would be fine, for two weeks, things were touch and go. I carried my Anointing Oil and Bible on every visit. As always, God placed wonderful people to assist during that difficult time.

The very first was a male nurse. He shared the same name as one of the disciples and my brother-in-law, the minister. Whenever I looked over, he looked away as if not to dare invade my privacy. He made small talk and told me that he had a fiancé. I thought what a lucky young lady. His spirit was comforting. I knew with care like that, recovery would soon follow. For him, it might have all been in a days work, but for me it was just what the doctor ordered during those initial moments.

The next nurse, stood out. Her imprint would be lasting. From the moment I saw her, I knew she was extra special. In my opinion she was one of God's Angels. Our spirits connected immediately. The only thing I can liken it to was when Elizabeth saw Mary during her pregnancy and John leaped in her womb. In her presence, I knew peace.

She was the consummate professional, but it was obvious that her belief was greater than the work she performed. Whenever she was near, my husband responded. Somehow he knew she was in his camp. She reassured me he would be fine. He remained in the coma and I remained prayerful. Both children were released from the hospital.

My son received several stitches in his ear and could not wait to get home to show his friends. The stitches were a hit with his school-aged peers, who had never had them there. My daughter suffered greater, including scarring and severe bruising. She was heavily medicated, and an emotional wreck, but held together like a champion. They returned home with family and friends to attend school. Each day the children and I prayed over the phone. I called with updates, discussed their day, allowed them to ask questions and then prayed.

During one of those prayer sessions, God informed me that my husband would wake up on the third day. I was so excited, certain he would be in ICU; eyes open waiting to see me. Then he could tell me about the journey he was obviously on. The entire time, he had a glow that both my daughter and I commented on.

Day two, still in a coma… Day three, deeper…seemingly worse not better. He was still in the coma on the third day. His eyes remained lifeless. Things did not look well. He was slipping away. I left the hospital to pray. During devotion, I kept wondering what was wrong. I was certain he would wake up on the third day. I did not think that I missed God. I continued to pray. I was sure that I needed to be in that room alone.

As days passed, faith diminished. It was no longer the coma that he needed to be delivered from, but from death. I needed a faith partner who would agree with me for the miracle. Since the hospital was in another city, the only individuals I felt had that level of faith were my daughter, son, his brother, and my best friend.

They were not there. My sister was positive, but had never taken a faith journey like this. I knew I needed someone who understood spiritual matters, the deep things of God. Everyone in their own way was as hopeful as they could be, but faith is the substance and the manifestation of deep desires. When things look impossible, sometimes it is hard to continue to believe. For me, the evidence would be his waking up in his right mind.

I did not want to offend family members or friends and briefly questioned it, but knew I was in no position to risk his life for emotions. This was not about feelings. Not even mine, because I was weary. This was about faith. The situation needed a miracle. I was certain of God's will and had no choice but to be obedient.

After some time in prayer, I called my brother-in-law, unaware that he was getting updates from his sister. I told him, 'He is still in the coma." I did not mention anything about faith levels but he said there were doubting spirits in the midst. He said I had to be stronger than ever because the enemy was trying to kill him and my faith was the only thing keeping the spirit of death from him. He told me that during his prayer time the Lord specifically instructed him to battle for his life. He said death was hovering over him and told me to remain strong. Things were not looking good.

At approximately the same time and unknown to me, my husband's friend was on the way to the hospital from our hometown, even though I told him not to come. Before leaving he said he had an urgency to pray and went back into the house and began to travail in prayer to the point of exhaustion. That friend arrived later before the next to the last visit. The medical reality was the longer the coma, the more adverse the affects on the brain. I informed his friend he had just missed visiting hour and the final visit was at 9:00 p.m. He said he would return then. We walked down what seemed to be the longest corridor of my life. When we got to his bed, he held back tears, although several got through. He looked at me and asked if I had any oil (Anointing Oil); instinctively I said yes and passed it to him.

"The Ram"

He began to anoint my husband and pray one of the most powerful prayers ever. That faith and focus was needed for the miracle. As he continued, he bound the spirit of death and forbid it from taking his life. He took authority as if Jesus had consumed his spirit. *The glow* came back several times throughout the process. There was *a powerful presence* like none I had ever felt. As he continued, ICU nurses peered curiously through the door.

He was the person of agreement necessary to pull the thing off. He was the chosen vessel to bring the miracle to pass. He was not needed before, but this was his appointed time. From the moment he walked in, I knew he was ready to battle anything that would prevent his buddy from awakening.

Remember if it is not God's will, no amount of faith can stop the inevitable, but thankfully, it was His will for my husband to live. When he finished, he took my hands, placed them on his chest, his on top, and said, "It is done." My buddy is waking up in the morning." God sent a friend with unwavering faith to touch, agree, and affirm His promise. He was the "plus factor." We walked arm in arm, back to the waiting room.

I was peaceful for the first time in a while. I knew "a change was coming." In the waiting room, he requested the family join in prayer. He prayed again with friends and family. We hugged and he said. "I'll see you tomorrow." I informed the night nurse that I was going to be at the hotel across the street and to call if anything changed. The nurse seemed glad that I was going to rest. He assured me he would call if there were any changes.

I went across the street to the hotel, showered and selected a decent outfit. I said, "My husband is waking up tomorrow. I need to be presentable. Until that point, I had no concern about my appearance, which was completely out of character. I paid little attention to what I wore, and did not care how I looked, nor who saw me. I just wanted this to be over.

For the first time since it happened, I did regular prayer and devotion for the very first time since the accident and slept peacefully. The alarm rang in time for the first visit. I got up certain he would wake up. I left the room around 4:30 a.m. in time for the 5:00 a.m. visit. I did not want anything to spoil the awakening. Little did I know that during the wee morning hours, his sister, convinced the night janitor to let her visit. She could not sleep and was determined to see her brother. She wept and I assume found peace, comfort, or strength she needed to remain strong. That morning, she arrived shortly after I did.

I was not in the waiting room long before someone called for me. The nurses were in process of changing shifts. When I got to the room, my favorite nurse was standing at the door saying, "He is trying to wake up!" She was beaming. During the entire comatose process, we were instructed to speak softly to keep from startling him, but now the nurse was saying to call loudly. She called his name and I joined in. He opened his eyes, smiled and passed out as if that one gesture took every ounce of energy he had. The nurse said to keep calling, so I did.

He said my name and knew who I was. He passed out again. He had the widest smile and the warmest glow ever. By now, his sister was in the room. And, my husband, a natural jokester was enjoying the attention. The nurse asked simple questions, like the day, birthday, etc. She asked if he knew who he was, the names of his children. He provided correct answers to all of her questions. When he named the children in order, beginning with his firstborn, our older son, I was very hopeful.

She told him he had been in an accident. He seemed surprised, and did not want to discuss that. He passed out again. The nurse allowed me to stay way past visiting hour. Because of the great news, most of the family arrived. His first words were, "Me and the Lord, we're tight." He repeated that over and over again... He wanted to know what happened to the party and why we were not celebrating. By then two of his brothers and his Mother had arrived. He looked at both and said their names. They held back tears.

The joy in that room was beyond anything one could imagine. There was a party all right and yes everyone did celebrate. During the awakening, my husband's friend arrived. We looked at each other nodding, yes. He spent time alone for whatever needed to transpire between them. Later, he informed me that my husband said that Jesus was at the foot of his bed. As soon as he said that, I was reminded that throughout the process, he would often move his feet from side to side in a playful manner.

I felt there was much more to the story. 1 Samuel 2:9 states that "He will guard the feet of his saints." The nurse continued to come in and out of the room giving various commands. She was as happy as the family. She said he would be fine. I began to tell everyone that the nurse was an angel. If she was not straight from God's kingdom, she was certainly one of his earth angels.

My husband continued to progress. Eventually, we came home to a more than three-year grueling process with major rehab and near financial ruin. Because of the accident and his profession, the game of life was over for him for a while. Rehab was four days a week, six hours a day. Initially, we both were required to attend. As time passed, I dropped him off in the morning and picked him up in the evening, with just enough time to get our son.

The extreme downside of a tragedy is that life goes on and so does most people, leaving you with fragments in hopes of piecing together something that resembles the life you once had. Most forgot that the toughest days were ahead. With any debilitating or long-term illness, finances are a major problem. We went without, not knowing how we would survive.

Medical bills depleted any assets. Insurance seems to cover what it wants to cover, but never the thing that can alleviate the most pressure. Our home was jeopardized with foreclosure. Still, I was amazed at the number of well meaning people who continued to come expecting to be treated like guests. Visits that created additional stress, work, hardship, and depleted energy and the little funds we had. Just getting through each day was challenging.

Most of the time, my husband was in and out. Those who visited seemed to believe he was further along in recovery than he was, perhaps their way of coping. The children and I, along with a few others knew otherwise. Everyone was excited about his progress, so we said very little. Most failed to realize the process was an ongoing, twenty-four hour job for our family.

Keeping the children grounded was a constant feat. Emotionally, they suffered and needed much more than I felt I could give. Rehabilitation wore heavily on the entire family--body, spirit and soul. Had I been in a traditional work environment, there is no way I could have managed. I stayed up at night to complete projects. I had one faithful writer who remained almost the entire time, assisting even when I could not afford to pay her any longer. Things that I considered normal before were now tremendous blessings.

My dear mother was a rare jewel, going the extra mile to attend to the children. She assisted with managing ongoing doctor appointments and helped me to juggle my work schedule. People rarely asked, "So how are you doing?" She and my father were among the few who seemed concerned about me. Since I am perceived as organized, perhaps some wanted to help, but did not know how. It amazed me that only a handful ever asked.

I realized that because of our lifestyle, people assumed things were well but we were far from it. Don't get me wrong, our life is not over the top, we have a long way to go, but we have been blessed. We worked hard, sacrificed, suffered, and took some huge risk throughout our journey. God is faithful. He gets credit for every good thing. Those who know me well know I am naturally hospitable. I love entertaining. But during a crisis, for the sake of the situation, come to help, or help by not coming. During that time, everything seemed burdensome. Things I once enjoyed became sources of stress. Visits add stress that further wears the caregiver. Still, I went out of my way to make sure he was in. Prior to visits, he got extra sleep so that he would be alert. I dressed him nicely, because he was naturally a sharp dresser, but he could care less. Worldly things seemed to frustrate him. After visits, he would sometimes sleep for two to three days, awakening only to eat.

I did not want others to see what the children and I knew. There were times that I watched his mannerism and wept. In the beginning there were many friends, family, and organizations that supported us, but as time went on, help dwindled to a very faithful few. I would never complain because I am thankful for every gesture, great or small. I understand people help from their point of reference, experience, or understanding. Some are good at accessing needs, others are not, but that does not diminish their heart.

Every kind gesture is a gift. Insightful, faithful friends assisted in various ways. They were God's greatest blessings. In the midst of it all, God never left us. There is no earthly reason why we did not fall apart, except for His hedge. When I look back, my soul still wonders, but deep down I know that God sustained us. Every aspect of our lives changed.

I assumed the role of head of household, sole breadwinner, chauffer, mother and father, caregiver, nurse, stabilizer, and more. Often I joked that my business gave us life, but his gave us our lifestyle. Little did I know how difficult life would be without his assistance. There were many things about our relationship that was flawed, but when it came to the children, we were the dynamic duo. We each had our roles and for the most part, played them to perfection. One of his greatest characteristics was being a great father. He was involved in every aspect of their lives. In over twenty years of marriage, I can count the number of times I prepared breakfast or made their lunch. He almost always did that.

He would never consider missing a parent-teacher conference, PTO meeting or the like. He did not mind driving them all over the world. Unlike me, he considered it quality time. He would often rearrange his schedule to pick them up from school and take them for an after school snack. My son was approaching the age where he needed dad more than mom. He desired "old dad" to return. I knew that no matter how good I was as a mother, he needed his dad to teach him how to be a man. Since they were both busy, staying on top of their schedules was a feat in itself.

No matter what happened, I tried to believe there was a solution. There usually was. I lived one day at a time. There was nothing to plan, because simple things like a decent meal were at stake. I was honest with the children about things that could affect them. I would give them the best scenario to the worst, but reminded them that God would ultimately decide our fate. Things we did without most people would never consider giving up.

For example, going without car insurance after such a horrendous accident. Somehow God hedged me and prevented me from accidents or receiving tickets. Right before it was time to renew my inspection sticker; I landed a contract and paid the policy in full for both cars for the entire year. That is grace. I have always been budget conscious (tight) and very creative with saving and spending money. In other words, "I can stretch a dollar."

Those skills came in handy. I also had parents who would "take care of things." They seemed to have a sixth sense and would always do things when I needed them most. Besides, I could always send the children there when food was too low, the house was too cold, or the power was out without question. There they could enjoy treats I could no longer afford. The children's faith was and still is amazing.

I knew the realities, the possibility of losing the house, having no money, and at times no lights, heat, or hot water. When the hot water heater broke at the coldest part of winter, and there was no money to repair it until winter was almost over. We boiled it for baths and dishes. I was at the point where everyone wanted me to do something, jump ship, move, and stop hoping in a hopeless situation. Most felt if I just moved into a smaller place that would help. What they did not realize was the house was the only thing that was normal for me. Moving at that time was too stressful and costly.

Most people cannot conceptualize real struggle where your basic existence is threatened, the kind where your next meal is at stake, when you are literally one step from homelessness and hopelessness. Once someone asked, about my cell phone which was funny, because keeping the regular one on was challenging. At one point, I even changed the number because of all the collection calls. At least I could control that. Besides, too many people had the number anyhow. I vowed not to give it out ever again. I had to survive and survival became the hardest part of the season.

Dark Tunnel

We did what we could to get by. Since he could not be left alone, the children would "Dad sit," so that I could do other things throughout or outside of the house. I did not dare leave the premise for fear of them not being able to handle him or of him falling and creating a worse scenario. I became the lawn guy and the pool guy since we could no longer afford them. Doing basic things like laundry was challenging because he needed around the clock care.

I worked in the evening once everyone was in bed. Thank God for e-business, a definite blessing. It increased productivity, helped me to control my time, and saved gas. As long as deadlines were met, no one really cared how. It was difficult for my husband to be in a position where he could not assist the family, but he maintained a positive outlook. Everything ran out except grace. At my darkest moments, I focused on the children. Living for them made me want to live. But there were times when depression consumed me where I fought for my sanity. I had some hopeless, forsaken, and forgotten periods, but believed things had to change.

My bouts of depression were so severe I had to fight to prevent myself from propelling into that distant place my grandmother once visited. I thought of her often and how difficult it must have been to cross the barrier into that realm and cried. I grieved for her pain, pain I felt. I understood the fragility of the mind and how thin the line is from sanity to insanity.

When I was really low, I often called my father. I am not sure if he knew or not, but he would always say the right thing. Still, there were times that I just wanted to give up. The enemy was relentless. His weapons were fierce. Not only did he attempt to kill my husband, but it seemed he wanted me dead too. I was in my own Gethsemane. Certainly death was better than this living hell.

God used a friend's call and the Holy Spirit to bring me out of that state. She called at one of the lowest points ever. Everyone was asleep. I was in a room alone weeping, ready, prepared for the end. Her timing was perfect. She prayed me out of that extreme bout of oppression that almost destroyed my hope. After that, I vowed that no matter what, the enemy would not win. The battle was not mine. It was greater than anything I could endure. And I had the promise, "That His strength would be perfected in my weakness." Boy, I was weak.

When bad things happened, a light always seemed to present itself. God always sent someone to assist like our neighbors who began to maintain our lawn at the precise time I felt I could no longer do it. Apparently, they discussed it because one did our right side, and the other maintained the left side. Neither ever mentioned it.

There was too much to do to stay depressed. I had to withstand the shakedown and allow God to work. My firstborn was going away to college and my younger returning to school. God provided in unusual ways. Checks out of the blue, bills suddenly paid, a friend who paid the mortgage—twice, healing in the midst of death, and protection from dangerous situations. My daughter being in the college of her choice is nothing shy of a miracle. Thankfully, that year my parents took care of back-to-school things and even covered unexpected fees for her tuition. Still money ran out and so did most people. I eventually sold a car, most jewelry, and anything else that could generate income. I was blessed to have some things to sell. Many facing the same sort of crisis may not.

Some of the greatest adventures are traveled on the loneliest highways. Struggle is not the worse thing that can happen. That's life. Everyone cannot endure what you have or go where you are going. God is doing something. Follow His prompting. Remove yourself from nay Sayers, no matter how close. You are trying to survive and anything or anyone that hinders that cannot be a part of your life.

Imagine the worse thing that can happen in your situation and determine what you will do if it does happen. Then no matter how difficult, move on to the best scenarios.

Once you face your fears, you relieve your mind and release energy to possibility solutions. Creativity is a great gift. The mind always provides insight to deal with the impossible. Making the right choice creates a divine flow of assistance to aide through your situation. Once you choose to survive, you live through it. "What doesn't kill you really does make you strong."

God grants miracles when you are at zero, expect Him to do wonders. Don't limit God, ever! Believe. Find scriptures that support your situation. Hold on to your professions and wait. No matter what happens you will be victorious. Stay in the race. Every season has a beginning and every season ends. Take care of yourself. Take time alone to think, to pray, to be. And, do simple things like exercise and drink plenty of water. Little things will aide you through the season.

When I think about the goodness of God it makes me weep. God provides and grants miracles. Many experience them firsthand. There is nothing like them. There is never any doubt when He has moved in your situation. Those who experience His power know this truth. You can only receive one with faith. No matter what the situation looks like, believe and never waver. Miracles are not just momentary blessings. They create lifelong changes affecting everyone connected to them. God will use your life as a testimony.

When you feel like giving up, He creates life from lifeless situations. No matter what, trust Him. Believe with your heart and soul. "If he brought you to it, He will bring you through it." Grow weary, but do not faint. Fall, but get back up. At your weakest point, God is strong and your weakness does not affect Him. Your season might be different from mine. Maybe yours is worse. Just remember, God is still in control. He does His best work at zero. If your situation is hopeless, you are a prime candidate for transformation. One touch from God can change everything in an instant. He is there waiting on you to make the right choice, so hold on, there is too much at stake for your faith to fail.

Chapter 4

Brittle Stalk

Sifting is a period when your nightmares come true. The apex of the season is the shakedown. Surviving it is paramount to your victory. When you are sifted, it is the devil, not God who desires you. The mere request is an honor you might not realize for years, decades, or perhaps until eternity. Prior to the season, you may have experienced a special fellowship with God, but now He seems distant. Now, your strengths will seem like weaknesses. As you face the shakedown, remember, some journeys involve you and God. Getting through the sieve is one of them.

The enemy does everything to shake, throw, toss, and rock your world to mess up your life. He is out to kill, steal, and destroy your Godly potential. He uses every available strategy to create a helpless, hopeless state. Sifting is not a one-problem event but a series of sudden endless challenges. No one has control over the season. Rational choices, that once seemed logical, are now irrational. Decisions are the "lesser of two evils."

Your life is at stake. There is little you can do because it is spiritual, beyond natural comprehension. Be still and trust that God is in control. Let Him push you through the sieve. Let go and let God be God. This is a test of survival. Completing the process determines how much life you get to live. The shakedown is fierce. You cannot endure it without God.

There is a saying, "The hallmark of a great man is not what he can live with, but what he can do without." Withstanding the shakedown requires creativity and strength. Things you once relied upon are useless now. You have one choice, to trust God. The enemy wants you to question everything. He wants you to forget that everything is in God's hand. He will not stop a minute before his time is up. He uses everything to destroy you.

When you are sifted you face huge mountains that overshadow your ability to see God. These giants haunt you day and night. What was once sane seems insane. No amount of praying seem to minimize the suddenlies. Your mountains, the goliaths are strategically there to place a wedge between you and God. They gain momentum while you shrink in their path. Rebuking them seems to summon more suddenlies. Suddenlies are there to create doubt and challenge your faith.

Trusting the seen or sane will get you in trouble. This is a time of blind faith and trust in God. Those who attempt to comfort you will do so from their perspective. Though well meaning, their advice is often rooted in their experiences and perspectives, or worse, their fears. When the season is too harsh, they use solutions for you to get out, rather than assist you through the process. Most give up on you all together and assume you must somehow deserve it. It is up to you to piece together the remnants from the sieve. Don't expect anyone to understand you now. As a matter of fact, expect the complete opposite. You may spiral into deep depression and despair. Or, spend hours trying to cope. At times, life is unbearable. Staying sane is insane. An insane asylum would be better than your living hell. At least then they might grasp that you are fighting for your life, and then no one will expect you to be normal. Then you can stop pretending you are okay. How can they miss your pain?

You have learned not to wear your problems on your sleeves and mastered the art of looking well when things are falling apart. If the "eyes are the mirror of the soul," yours are cloudy. Well-meaning friends and family remain clueless. The reality is no one understands. They are supposed to know you, yet they miss the mark, not one time, but every time. They could never imagine the constant dread, let alone survive it. You are your worst enemy, your own worst critic.

The accuser assaults you through negativity, paranoia, and depression. Instead of acting like God, you pick up traits of the very one who is seeking to destroy you. The enemy will not stop. He will use everything to weaken you. He reminds you of every fault. He loves using your pre-saved behavior to condemn you. Reminding you of the past is an easy path to destruction. The enemy knows many things about you and uses them to distort the truth, leaving a hazy version of the promises of God.

Once truth is clouded, deception is easier. He tried it with Jesus, so don't think he won't try it with you. He will remind you of your alcoholism, drug addiction, lust, perversion, insecurity, socialism, materialism, greed, and even your righteousness, to weaken you. He will use everything to prevent you from completing the process. You might even be presented with the very person or thing that is the source of your isms to further weaken you.

The devil will even use Christianity to throw you off track. He will encourage you to attend every church gathering, prayer meeting, or conference at the expense of your family, prayer life, work, or other responsibilities. Balance is the key to a healthy life. The enemy overloads you at the expense of your well-being. He wants you to continue in unworthiness. He wants you to believe you are too far-gone for God to care. He reminds you at every opportunity.

This is the time to get your fight back and remind him of his future, where he was defeated. Do not be deceived God is always glorified. Things the enemy attempts for harm, God makes good. The devil want your "if I coulda, woulda, shoulda's" to become personal mantras. If your vision is clouded you cannot focus. The enemy would rather you forget what God has already delivered you from. Jesus paid the ultimate price for the worse things you could ever do. Besides, the devil never desires someone incapable of producing a harvest.

Farming is a good example of the process. Good farmers expect good crops and good Christians should expect a good outcome. Those who are obedient and faithful should expect a harvest. Wheat farmers anticipate good crops as soon as they plant seeds. Though they plant during the fall, they expect a harvest by summertime.

Between seasons farmers rely on the process to work, while expecting a good outcome. As they wait, they experience fall, with beautiful colors; turn into the bitterness of winter, that is cold, dry, and barren; in hopes of getting to spring where life blossom again. Like wheat, you must endure the process to get to your harvest.

As they wait, often they see very little. Sprouts may grow, but overall the plant lies dormant. There is little chance of a harvest then. It is not time, and timing is everything. In some instances, the goal is merely surviving the harsh season. Winters are when farmers are faithers. They rely on provisional blessings to get through the season. They know weathering every storm is the best hope for a great crop.

Your harvest may be hidden during winter, but underneath something explosive is happening. Brave the cold and have faith. You may not see anything but the process is working some things out. Farmers wait for the evidence of the things they have sown, even though they may only see remnants of their crops. Farmers work in preparation of harvest time. Right now, it might be cold, dry, and brittle, but wait for a change. Look beyond the present season and anticipate your harvest.

Wheat farmers want dry, brittle stalks. At the hottest, driest point, when it seems the stalks are good for nothing, is when they are broken and the seed retrieved. Stalks must be dry and parched so that they can be stored without spoiling. Dryness is when things seem hopeless. The brittle, fragile stage is your brokenness. If not handled properly permanent damage occurs. The sticks seem useless, but an explosive harvest is inside. At the driest most brittle point, the farmer breaks and retrieves the seed.

When broken improperly, the stalks are ruined, and the good seeds scatter. Christians need to understand that unlike wheat farmers, God locates scattered seeds, those invisible to the naked eye. Nothing is lost with Him. To get to your seed, you must be broken. God wants to break you, but gently. He wants to retrieve the seed to assure there is enough for an explosive harvest. In many ways the farmer's method can be compared to God. He knows exactly where, when, and how much pressure is needed to break and retrieve the great seeds that are inside of you. He knows the importance of getting to the good seed where the harvest is.

Once the brittle stalks are retrieved, the stubble is mixed into the soil. It kills any weeds that hinder growth and saves soil moisture for the next wheat crop. It nourishes and kills at the same time. It destroys anything that would hinder another crop. Farmers know when the process is successfully followed, it almost always produce a harvest. Christians should know that following God's word does the same.

Sometime, harvesting takes years because the farmer might have to try several parts of the ground to determine the best soil. Disappointment and failure are all a part of the process, yet he

> *When you are dry and brittle, God gently breaks you and retrieve your seed.*

remains hopeful, knowing, he will reap if he stays faithful to the process. Stakes are high for producing a good first crop. Extra special care is needed because a good first crop is the key to getting seeds for future harvests. The enemy wants you stripped of sustenance. He prefers you in parched ground. God built you to weather your barren season, and can even bless your stubble. When there are extra seeds, that means the farmer planted in good soil. From then on, a good harvest can be expected. If the farmer attends to the field and follow the process, he can expect a harvest. When you attend to your faith, you too can expect a great crop.

That is why the first crop is the most difficult. That crop is the costliest because it is the biggest failure or the biggest payoff. It produces for generations. Speak to any self-made millionaire. They will tell you the first million was their hardest. The same is true of your harvest. From a good crop you get seed for more fruit. The pioneers, the dreamers, the risk takers, the first, always pay the heftiest price, but they also make the path easier for those who follow.

You are never blessed for yourself but to be a blessing. Every good seed is rewarded. You might not see the results right away, but keep nurturing your soil. Trust God to sustain and protect your brokenness. At the appointed time, you will reap a bountiful harvest. The fight is not natural. This is not the time to think like the enemy, instead learn to think and act like God.

Satan knows humans have been given the ability to choose and the power that comes through that decision. He has never been privy to free will but can certainly impact yours. He is constantly waging war on your thoughts because he knows if you are mentally weary you cannot be productive. Your mind is the central command station, the nucleus.

Headaches, stomachaches, ulcers, rashes, hives, insomnia and depression, most often are attributed to mental strain. A poor diet or lack of exercise diminishes capacity. Over or under eating robs the body of much needed nutrients to fight or endure challenges. Cravings like coffee, chocolate, and sweet, or salty foods could be indicators that you are not in your best condition. Instead of eating more of the things that are unhealthy, supplement your diet with energy and natural foods like fruits and vegetables, with lots of water. It is amazing how a simple glass of water makes you feel. Extra doses of natural vitamins might not hurt either.

When you are sifted, it is important to eat, exercise, pray and meditate daily on God's word. Get as much rest as much as possible. Stress takes a heavy toll on the mind, and will eventually wreak havoc on the body. When you are sifted, you may feel caring for self is a luxury you cannot afford. But, do not neglect anything that fuel or energize you. It is easy to destroy a body operating with a weak command center. During difficult periods, soundness of mind is critical for divine insight and wisdom. This is not scientific, but common sense, a commodity that is often neglected.

Take a walk or find a still quiet place to clear your head each day. Little things will aide you in getting through the sieve. The shakedown is fierce and cannot be survived without God. Trusting God is easy when things are well, but try having that same hallelujah when you lose a loved one, a child, a parent or a spouse. Suppose you discover some debilitating illness. What if your house is foreclosed on, your car is repossessed, your business fails, your children stray, your spouse is unfaithful, or worse. Can you withstand the shakedown, or do you wimp out on God? Does your hallelujah become a small, distant whimper instead of a shout? Sifting separates the minors from the majors. Things that do not make it through the sieve are necessary losses.

Many do not withstand the shakedown, because they give up before receiving the promise. They become overwhelmed with doubt and allow their present condition to dictate their faith. They make permanent change during a temporary season. They trust in the seen, instead of trusting in the only sure thing--God's ability to deliver. Jesus prayed, your victory is assured, but you have a choice. Trust God when zero is the only option. He is the God of good success. He cannot fail. God knows you will succeed. In due season, you will realize the power within. You may question, but never doubt God. Seasons change. Do not give up.

> *It is all about perspective. What do you see, a big problem or a big God?*

Sifting removes impurities from your life. Since you have little control, this is the place where you learn complete dependency on God. Like a child, you learn that if He does not nourish and sustain, you die. He provides bread to strengthen you throughout the season. The process may seem unending, but do not attempt to go through it without Him. Every day becomes a new opportunity to trust Him.

When I was sifted, I suffered severe insomnia and could never nap more than a couple of hours each night. At first, I found it frustrating, unbearable at times. I added to my woes by worrying about how tired I would be the next day. At some point, I decided that instead of brooding to develop a "to do" list. When I could not sleep, I would pull out the list and get busy. Things I had put off forever, I began to complete. This made life easier and more productive. One of those things included writing this book.

Oh there were things on the list I dreaded, but also some wonderful things. I cleaned the garage, did loads of laundry, or cleaned the interior of my car. I prepared boxes for charity picks ups, read and answered mail, wrote letters, painted, and decorated. I even cleaned out the fridge, made grocery lists and paid bills. Since I could no longer afford manicures or pedicures, I became proficient at my own. When I look back my life was better organized and less cluttered. I created many systems I still use today. I did something else. I created a blessing list. Little ways I could somehow bless others. Many things on the list were soul lifters, like an overdue promise to redecorate my son's room.

Although I did not feel I had much to offer, thinking of things to do for others prevented me from idolizing my problems. Since things were in such an extreme state, I had to be creative. Every insurance policy lapsed, retirement was depleted, savings was gone, and the house was in foreclosure. Bank accounts were either closed or had a couple of dollars. Many of our valuables were sold for basics like food and utilities, but thank God we had something to sell. I could barely keep food on the table or gas in the car, but there were cars, both paid for, that was a blessing.

Blessing Lists

I was certain that you reaped what you sowed and since we needed money, I had to come up with innovative ways to sow those seeds. I had little but trusted God to guide the process. To bridge the gap between my ongoing challenges and unending suddenlies I became involved giving my time, talents, and skills to benefit others.

Some things that I normally charged for, I did for free. I assisted in creating two non-profit organizations during that time. One I still donate my services to. God was faithful, showing me what to do, when, and how. The process was amazing.

He would place certain people on my heart that seemed to have no apparent need. Others merely needed a visit, ride, telephone call, card, candy bar, or a hug. I cleaned out drawers and closets, gave things to families and organizations that could better utilize them. For instance, a friend's college-aged daughter, an avid photographer, camera was stolen. I offered her the use of my 35 mm. Initially, I thought she could use it until she got another one, but when I saw her with it, I knew it was hers. Besides photography was one of her gifts. She had won several national awards. I knew she would use the camera wisely.

There was no money for birthdays or holidays, I selected favorite things of mine as gifts. Many who knew our situation questioned how I could afford them, but the looks of love on most were worth it. And, I needed as much seed as possible in the ground. My husband could no longer drive so several people used the extra car. At least two people, whose situations were worse, lived with us. We were honest about the financial situation. As long as we had a place, they could stay.

Because of the time it took to manage the household, work, and care for my husband, there were things I could no longer manage efficiently. One of those guests contributed and assisted with things that made the entire household better. Unlike the horror stories I had heard and even experienced before with live-ins, they were wonderful.

When you are sifted, be creative. Sow into the lives of others. Find something you can do consistently during the season like mowing the lawn, providing lunch money for a small child, purchasing laundry products, a gas card, cleaning supplies, or snacks for younger children. Perhaps you are able to something larger like a month's rent, a large bill, a car note, insurance payment, or as one dear friend did, pay the mortgage.

Another, an extremely highly paid professional maintained my hair. Because of all of the stress mine was thinning and balding. That gesture was a lifesaver that preserved my self-esteem. Thanks to her, my hair grew back healthier than before. Once, I remember having only $20.00. Credit cards were not even a thought. God specifically led me to give half to a particular person. Later, I found she needed gas to pick up money she was borrowing for an emergency. In case you were unsure of the severity of the situation, keep in mind that was the only money for the upcoming week.

When you sense that someone is being sifted, don't buy luxury items over basics like food, clothing, and household supplies. Pay a bill, purchase a grocery gift card, gas gift card, or offer to do something special for younger children. If possible, take the sick person and keep them over night, a half-day or even a couple of hours is a reprieve for the caregiver. That gesture can keep them sane. If you are uneasy, do or send things anonymously. They will appreciate it and God will bless your efforts.

Don't expect them to ask, because most people suffer in silence. Sow some seeds. The smallest thing you do might be the greatest area of need. Giving from excess is a blessing; a position God wants all the saints in, but giving from lack is a sacrifice few are willing to make. There must be an even greater reward for that. My list helped me to identify a person each week to bless. God always confirmed my selections. Sometimes the thing was so small and simple it shocked me, but it was always the right thing.

God continued to place others in our path who were less fortunate. I learned that no matter how difficult the trial, there is always one worse. And, "It is more blessed to give than to receive." A dear friend puts it this way, "Don't let anyone rob you of your blessings." God honors effort. I received more than I could ever give. I began to thank God and learned the meaning of "widow mites giving."

Timing was crucial because meeting a need at the appropriate time is the best gift of all. Throughout the process I received wonderful blessings, including quiet time during those wee morning hours. I often sat and watched the sunrise. That stillness is still one of the things I treasure most.

There are times when I schedule at least two or three sleepless nights. I look forward to completing some project uninterrupted. I savor a fresh cup of coffee and adore communion with the Lord. I praise and thank the Creator for the miracle of the morning, at the dawn of a new day.

There is a harvest in you. God ordained it. Your suffering cannot overshadow it. The shakedown is about perspective. Who do you see more of, your problem or your God? Look at the magnitude of God and problems diminish in comparison. Whatever you need, He provides. When you look back, you will be amazed at the obstacles you survived. Be faithful. Run the race. Be a winner. Your suffering will end. "You will understand it better by and by." Imagine God sitting on the throne applauding each time you overcome a challenge.

God has given you the keys to the kingdom. Use them and survive. As you near the end of the shakedown, you will feel a certain excitement in your spirit. You will get through the sieve. Notice words within the definition of sieve like **impure, separate, coarse, strain, force, push,** and **purification**. All of these words are relative to the season.

> *An instrument with a meshed or perforated bottom used to remove the impure so that only the pure remains. A sieve separates coarse matters from finer parts of loose matter. A sieve is used for straining liquids, wheat, and flour. A sieve has one circular frame and fine meshes or perforations. The hall-*

mark of a sieve is that force, great or small pushes the substance through the sieve for purification.

Sifting occur when impure particles that are too large are shaken, broken, and forced through the mesh part of the sieve. The one operating the sieve is the sifter. When you are sifted, the devil may hold, tear, and separate, but God refines for the harvest. In other words, God retains control of the process. He allows the enemy to shake it to remove the coarse parts.

It might be difficult to understand that the present suffering does not compare to the glory ahead. The light at the end of the tunnel may seem dismal. One storm calms quickly giving way to another. Do you recall Job? Remember, there were parameters, things that no matter what remained off limit. The devil was given guidelines for the attack of Job's life, but no matter what he did, he could not kill him. He did as much as he could to get Job to curse God, but Job remained faithful.

Mrs. Job on the other hand began to live under her circumstances. Like most, she was only human. She absorbed the realities of her circumstances and could not understand how the God of Abraham, Isaac, and Jacob could allow that kind of suffering to such a righteous man. She must have felt that if theirs was the result of righteous living, then what was the point? She questioned God. As a matter of fact, she did not want anything to do with Him and wanted her husband to take that same position.

Imagine the same Job, whose wife said, "Curse God and die," was the very one who had all of those children, grandchildren, and great-grandchildren.

She lived to receive blessings because of her connection to Job and because of his connection to God. Can't you imagine Mrs. Job in the town square saying, "I don't know how we made it through the sieve, but we did. Those were some dark days. There were times when I knew death should certainly be better." Her testimony not only convinced it convicted. Those who heard already knew their situation. It was the talk of the village. Her testimony made it easier for those facing trials to endure. Her victory was a witness to everyone she encountered.

Nothing could replace the lost children but God did not leave her barren. I am sure that Mrs. Job went on and on about how honored and esteemed she and Job were. I am certain that all of her children called her blessed. Their season changed them forever. They had a limp and thorn. They could never forget what God brought them through. They were probably better parents, better to each other, more attentive to their health, more faithful with their finances, more philanthropic and better servants the second time around.

They learned to live each day to the fullest. God gave them double for their trouble The Job's had memorial stones. When faced with difficulties, their children remembered the story and persevered. If God restored The Jobs who birthed and lost ten children, how much more will He do for you? God repairs, refines, and restructures. Allow Him to make your crooked matters straight. You have been purchased with blood. That blood makes you a joint heir with all rights and privileges. Walk in the air as an heir. Your birthright entitles you to some things. You are supposed to live the abundant life.

Don't allow your present situation to cause you to live beneath your potential. Your Father is a King. You should live royally. You are an heir; receive the promises He has for you. At the appointed time and not a moment sooner, you will receive your crown. Your time might seem far, but it will come. Hold on and dream big. Maybe you are like Joseph, a young man with a huge vision who was distracted by the pitfalls of life.

God knows the perfect time for your vision. Had God allowed Joseph to birth his dream before the appointed time, he would not have been in the place to deliver the very family who mocked him, nor be able to assist the many who would have perished during the famine (Gen. 37). God allowed mistreatment, envy, and jealousy within his own family to force him from his comfort zone, placing him in his position of destiny.

Their limited vision placed him in a horrific position, changing everything he had ever known. As time passed, Joseph matured to understand the dream was not just for him. Their betrayal, proved to be his (and theirs) greatest blessing. Even though his dream was accurate it was not time. The right thing, for the right reason, at the wrong time, is wrong.

Timing is critical when executing a vision. Joseph matured to understand that everyone does not desire to see beyond today. He had to learn to control his enthusiasm, especially around those with limited vision. He was not mature enough to understand the need to control his tongue, or that those with limited views can seldom embrace the vision of another. He had to learn those lessons in the sieve.

A big vision will alienate and create dissention especially among those you love most. Over time Joseph matured, persevered, and received godly insight to fulfill his destiny. He had to wait for the appointed time. As heirs, you must wait to inherit the palace. The pitfalls may temporarily stop you, but in the end they make you stronger. They bring you to a greater dependency upon God.

When the kairos moment arrives nothing will be able to stop the blessings. The vision really is for an appointed time, make it clear, make it plain, and make it happen. The season of vision, provision, and preparation breaks you so that you can inherit your rightful place and claim your inheritance. Let the Bible be your standard. All of the answers lie between its pages. Avoid meaningless chitchat that wastes time, instead look for moments to be alone with God Pay attention to any word confirming any revelations. This could be Pastors, books, friends, music, art, or some other divinely inspired thing.

The Word is the strength needed to withstand the suddenlies. Fill your mind with it. God never abandons you. The sieve separates the test from the testimony. The story is to glorify God. God does not get glory unless you complete the process. Then your testimony will transform your life and the lives of others. You are chosen to help others survive. You will look back in amazement at the obstacles He brought you through.

The enemy wants you to stop "three feet from your blessing." Don't live without fulfilling your purpose. Don't be afraid, Jesus prayed. You will complete the process. If you were incapable of producing a great harvest, the enemy would have never requested you. Remember perspective, it is about perspective. Who do you see, the problem or God? Look at the magnitude of God and your problems diminish in comparison. You may see bitter days, but endure. You are chosen with a divine purpose. He knows what is inside. He will strengthen you. Stay in the race until you hear, "Well done my good and faithful servant." And because Jesus already prayed, your faith will not fail.

Chapter 5

The Shakedown!

The scene is explosive, episodic in proportion. "Peter, Satan desires to have you to sift you as wheat, but I am praying that your faith will not fail." Just as Jesus predicted, Peter denied Him. On the third crow, Jesus looked directly into his eyes. Peter must have felt condemned but Christ saw no condemnation. Because of the denial that staunch disciple, the rock thought it was over. Imagine the pain.

Peter thought he was better than that. He walked with Jesus, watched His miracles and healing powers, and knew Him intimately. Surely, he would never deny Him. But, Peter had a particular problem with pride and self-control and his shakedown was inevitable. He had to be broken and forced through the sieve before fulfilling his destiny.

If suddenlies are the surprises that force you into a sifted season, the shakedown is what you must endure before coming out. Unlike suddenlies that just happen where there is little to no control, the shakedown is a part of the process that you must choose to survive. The challenges that forced you into the sieve create the ultimate shakedown where survival becomes the harshest part of the season.

You must survive the shakedown or you will wither and die. This is the part of the season that Jesus warned Peter about when he said, "I am praying that your faith will not fail." This is a fierce battle that cannot be won in the natural. Without supernatural assistance, you are doomed to defeat. But, when you hold on during the shakedown, victory is assured. You may be scarred, bruised, broken, and brittle, but you will survive.

Christ knew the season was necessary to destroy everything that would hinder Peter's ministry. Peter's name meant stable, reliable, rock solid, but those characteristics were not fully developed at that point of his life. Christ wanted him to survive the shakedown because He knew what was inside. Envision Christ reminding Peter, "This was the shakedown I warned you about, but you will survive." Making it through meant becoming a vessel God could use.

Peter's sifting was part of a divine plan. He came to know that any power he had was because of the one he served. Great leaders like him can get caught in their own hype when it is God's Anointing that gives them power, position and prestige. Great power is detrimental without humility. Often, many dynamic leaders fall because they refuse to bow to the one who raised them up. A man who needs and require glory is a crutch to himself and those around him. Continuous intimacy with God is necessary especially during successful times. It is easy to become prey when everything is well.

Success can create false securities and set up walls that collapse. Use successful periods to remain humble. It is only by the grace of God that you do whatever you do anyhow. No matter what God is preparing you for, when you receive it, glorify Him. That must be learned before harvest time. Leaders must be certain they are serving and relying on God.

Some seasons are meant to end quickly. Others are prolonged for lasting harvest potential. Whatever season you are in, "blossom where you are planted." Make the most of your situation. No matter how difficult life becomes remain thankful. Press on in spite of your feelings and your circumstances.

Negative feelings will stop blessings. Great things happen to people with a positive outlook. They "take a licking and keep on kicking." Their stories about blessings are amazing. Some of the most successful people ever are adversity busters. No matter what happens, they believe they will be okay. They get down but never count themselves out. They deal with adversities because they know; no man can escape it so they make the most of it. They believe at the end of every great challenge is victory.

God does not care about your location or condition. He comes into places most would never consider, just for you. Your hog pen is not a deterrent. The stench of your slop does not cause him to turn up his nose. He will go to any length to save you.

Peter still had failure issues and the denial was the lowest point of his life, but Jesus wanted Peter to be reassured by His love. No matter how he felt, he had already been forgiven.

God knows your dry, brittle, parched places. His love knows no boundaries except your willingness to receive it. Jesus knew what was inside and so did the devil. The devil does not request wimpy saints; he wants saints with long-term harvest producing seeds.

The same seed that God desires to build upon is the one satan want to destroy. The devil wants a soul saving, delivering, healing, transforming, powerful individual. Destroying your faith makes his job easier. Satan is the author of lies. He wants to keep you in your past so that you will not realize the great future God has. He wants your pain to prevent you from moving into your blessed place. He does not want you to believe that if you just touch His hem, you can get to HIM. He does not want you to believe that your faith makes you whole. He would rather beat and break you until you give up. The saints God wants to build upon are prime targets. Do not allow him to rob you of your mission.

You are a joint heir. Put on your crown and bid your blessings they will come. "Call those things that be not as though they are." Harvest time depends upon you, not the enemy. Don't let him tamper with your soil (soul). God knows His creation and the harvest you need to produce while on earth. Don't allow your past, hurts or pains to hinder your crop. There are great seeds inside. No matter how hard, continue to believe. God knew when he placed you in your mother's womb the conditions you would endure and their ripple effect. Don't' allow His divine will to be disrupted by your challenges.

Wise choices will make the path easier. Wrong ones will cause additional difficulties. Some bad choices result from associations, familiar connections, or generational factors. Those connections often force saints to suffer through seasons because of the decisions of others. For example, a husband's bad choice as spiritual head of household will affect his entire family, perhaps for generations.

Those who fail to see the significance of their Godly role bring undue heartache and despair into the lives of those who need them. A wife who makes poor decisions will particularly impact her home and her children. Selfish parents, who live at the expense of their children, create an atmosphere for them to choose poorly. At some point, adult children are accountable for changing destructive patterns but the road is often difficult.

Parents who acknowledge wrongs open the door to new relationships. No matter how irreparable, most children love their parents unconditionally. One word of caution to parents who have lived selfishly, do not demand things from them that you did not do yourself. Accept the relationship on their term, their way. Trust God to heal and restore. As adults, they can choose a life with or without you. Sadly, the effects can be seen in any nursing home in the country.

Some of the loneliest seniors were the worse parents. In those final years, instead of being cared for by loved ones they are cared for by strangers just doing a job. Unlike those who must have ongoing care, they rarely, if ever, receive visitors. Still, Christ can heal any relationship. There is always the opportunity to make the right choice. Be the bigger person--forgive.

Some parents fail to understand that children are gifts who did not ask to come into the world. Parents have an obligation to give their children the best they have to offer, and yes, at their own expense. Whether you have a little or a lot, love is unlimited and is needed most. Parents, please, once you have children, do your best to rear them the way that God would.

What if you knew every decision you made, good or bad, would affect them, how would that altered your choices? Take advantage of the gift that even Angels do not have, the power to choose. Make your choices count. If you were not a good parent, acknowledge that and apologize to your children, no matter what their age. Acknowledging wrong create pathways to a brighter future.

It may be painful, but remember, harvest time is worth it. Besides, your actions could affect the relationship of any grandchildren who are naturally more loving. This does not mean that children should dishonor their parents, that should never happen. If most knew better, they would have done better.

You may not love your parents but you are obligated to honor them. Without them, you could not be on the planet. When you know better you are obligated to do better. Whatever it takes, take the steps, if not for you, for your children. "The journey of a thousand miles begins with one step." One person does make a difference. You could be that person.

Through Jesus, the door is always accessible. Don't allow what you missed to negatively affect your children. "Step up to the plate" and make every decision count.

Wouldn't it be a shame to find out that the only thing preventing you from fulfilling your destiny was you? Oh, you can probably live a decent life, but don't you want God's best? Use your power to choose wisely. Seek His guidance and end up in the place God has for you.

Whether sifting, separating, picking, or pruning, the concept is the same. If you pick apples from an apple tree, before you sell them, you have to pick through them to make sure there are no spoiled ones, because one rotten apple does affect the whole bunch. A homemaker cannot just toss clothes in the washing machine all at the same time and expect positive results. For those who have inadvertently washed a red sock in the midst of all white clothing, you get the picture.

Right now, your night might be extra long, but hold on, your morning may be right behind it. Don't be afraid of your trial. Jesus prayed. Your victory is assured. Can you endure to receive it? Your reward might be in the midst of your present trouble, the one you cannot see past. Hold on and endure. Do not give up. Remember, "It is not the swiftest, nor the fastest, but the one who stays in the race who wins." God allowed the enemy to sift you; yet, He retained control of the sieve to carefully maneuver all circumstances including evil for His ultimate purpose.

Human beings do not know specifics regarding spiritual laws. Even the most knowledgeable can only understand it through natural means. Knowledge given by the Holy Spirit will elevate your understanding. Still, you are dealing with spiritual things in a natural body. Apparently spiritual laws allow the enemy to target certain individuals at specific times. God pointed Job out as an example of a righteous man, but allowed him to suffer. The enemy seems to have a certain amount of time to shake you down and must wage a fierce war in hopes that you quit. Do not be deceived, his goal is for you to give up on yourself, but more importantly on God. The only way the enemy wins is if you stop believing.

Remember, Jesus continues to intercede that your faith does not fail. Rejoice knowing He is telling the Father to provide help for you to get through. There is a process for everything. Sifting develops that distinct portion of you character that is most like God's. It refines and separates the tears from the wheat. God does not allow sifting because He enjoys seeing you suffer, but because He is a good Father. He knows your divine role in this great game of life. Maybe that is why you are at this point now, so that He can get to the unique crop only you can produce.

You might lose sight of the seed but God always knows its whereabouts. Trust Him. He can deliver. God want the greatness inside. He knows your capabilities. Today your circumstances might seem impossible, but God has already made provisions. Before the earth was formed, God knew you. He knew your birth circumstances, family, physical features, and characteristics. He knew which things would cause you to become brittle and frail, but He also knew what was inside. You have already endured what most cannot imagine, and survived. At the appointed time, and not a moment sooner God will deliver.

Remember, the devil made a special request and he does not ask for just anyone. God, not the devil said yes. God would have never given permission for your demise. He sent his son Jesus to experience the harshest part.

Sifting forces you to surrender—to let God be God. Trust Him to guide you to a hope-filled future. Let him gently break your brittle stalk. He knows how much pressure is needed to retrieve the great seeds within. At the appointed and acceptable time, you will reap. God sees your brokenness and knows there is too much at stake for your faith to fail.

Chapter 6

Make Me Whole

Imagine being shaken, tossed, and thrown to begin the process again. That is what sifting is like. The shakedown removes everything unholy, impure, or unworthy of the destiny awaiting you. The process is not complete until you develop complete trust and dependency on God. It is necessary before producing a great crop. Purification creates hunger for God like never before. It provides a view of things from a supernatural perspective.

Purification listens with the heart, not the head. It dies to self, flesh, ego, pride, haughtiness and anything that hinders the path to God. It yields and submits to the Father. "Oh to be a pawn in the Lord's hand," allowing Him to move you across the chessboard of life. No matter how fierce or challenging the game, you are certain to hear checkmate. Purification develops that distinctive essence of your character that is most like God.

Sifting changes your perspective, causing you to see things as God does. Your outlook is more Christ-like. When you begin to see through His eyes, agape love overtakes you. You learn that behind each human being is a powerful set of circumstances forming the fabric of their life. You measure man through God's eyes where everyone is equal. Through the process you find your created purpose.

You were created for something greater than yourself.

> There may be no apparent fruit in your life.

Purification helps to find it. Now that you are refined, mountains that would never given way, crumble at your presence. You mastered the test. You have a supernatural advantage. You survived the shakedown. With that comes new vision. When you experience hurt and pain, you understand there is a greater power at work. Remember, negative people or situations are there to teach you something to aid in your journey. Until you grasp the lessons they remain, but once you pass through the sieve, suddenly, they are gone.

When you are sifted, removing unhealthy people or things isn't always easy because areas in your life dry up and become fruitless. Lack of fruit is one indicator that something is not quite right. Even if it is as simple as "the devil desired to sift you." God want fruit bearing saints who understand kingdom building principles. He needs saints who understand that overflow flows into the lives of others. Remember, Job was sifted for being righteous. Sifting is never for you, but those connected to you.

Miracles are often the result for your trouble. They occur to let everyone know God is powerful. A touch from Him can change any situation in an instant. The criteria for most miracles seem to be an impossible situation; a challenge against God's ability to perform; everyone knows; lives are changed; and, God is glorified. If there is still an option your situation is not ready for a miracle. When God meets zero, expect them.

Miracles are signs, omens, difficulties, or wonders, creation, or novelty. Miracles confound traditional knowledge. Surviving give hope to others. Your situation can inspire them to stay in the race. Just because you are being sifted does not mean you do not have a great seed. Lives are meant to bear good fruit. God wants to produce through your life. In order for God to bring out the best, sometimes He allows a dry, brittle, barren season. Endure the process. When you come forth you will be as pure gold.

Like produces like, and whatever is sown, you eventually reap. So whatever you need most, sow it. Fruit is fruit, and great fruit can only come from a great seed. No one can obtain God-like qualities without the process. To be right spiritually is a process.

When the harvest is spiritual, use spiritual means to obtain it. Purification gets you there. It teaches you to prune things that affect your harvest. It develops discipline in the things of God. Never underestimate the power of prayer, fasting, or meditation. Praying, in the spirit, is another way to obtain your harvest. Spiritual prayer edifies and give insight into the mind of God. It is one weapon that all Christians can have. Do whatever it takes to become a fruit bearer.

Those who reap greatly in the Kingdom have sown and suffered greatly. Any material gain is a by-product of their endurance. Hard times are often the vessels that create change. A purified person is not bound. They are free from things that hinder God's work in their lives. They are governed by supernatural instead of natural laws. A person who has gone through the sieve has faith beyond comprehension. They have learned to be quiet when God speaks because what they say may appear insane or irrational. Purified lives produce and become the reason for living.

Never discount a person because of their present state. Unless you know what seeds they've sown, you could miss their harvest by looking at what seems obvious. Before purification, Apostle Paul was the infamous Saul, who persecuted Christians. He is a perfect example of a purified soul.

After his conversion, he pressed forward to his high calling. He lived fully and completely for Christ. Once converted, all was not well for Paul. He faced many trials. He was shipwrecked, bitten by poisonous snakes, beaten, and jailed. Nevertheless, he knew that it was not he who lived, but the Christ in him. Paul never questioned the great works he did because he knew they were of God.

He lived a supernatural life after his conversion, something he could have never accomplished in the natural. In the end, he was certain that he fought the good fight of faith. Yet, along the way, he experienced fruitless periods and harsh trials. Harvest time cannot occur without it. Fruitless periods could last days, weeks, months, years, and yes even decades.

The longer you are in the sieve, the greater your harvest potential. If you wait, you will receive a harvest because of your connection to the Blessed One. Being connected is critical. If you are around during harvest time you will receive something. Do not allow present day crisis to prevent you from your blessing. Underneath your challenge, a strong root might be forming. Although it cannot be seen, deep down lies a bountiful harvest. What if God had failed to see the fruit bearing potential in Abraham the moon worshiper, Jacob the deceiver, Moses the murderer, Paul the persecutor, David the adulterer, Rahab the whore, wishy-washy Peter, Jeremiah the crybaby, hard-headed Jonah, or dead, stinking Lazarus?

Look beyond what you see to discern the type of crop God is creating in your life. Just because you don't see it, does not mean it is not there. If you have sown, you will reap. Like Ruth, God will position you to receive favor. Being in the right place at the right time may be all you need to receive your breakthrough. In the meantime do everything in your power to affect your situation. Then be still and trust God.

Those who have experienced God's transforming power know miracles. The glory is in the story and testimony, in the test. Great leaders whose lives are fruit-filled often suffer tremendously in the sieve. Their stories are filled with hardships, challenges, losses, or worse. There is a saying, "no story, no glory" and "no test, no testimony." Fruit bearers endure.

To ensure victory, stay before the throne. Man may fail, but God never does. Once you understand who you are in Christ, you obtain wholeness. Getting there might mean a wrestling match like Jacob's with a name change, but it is worth it. You are a new and improved model.

Thank God for the season. Without it you would not be who you are today. Accept your limp. Praise God for it because it is your memorial stone, a reminder of God's strength. Whatever happens is a part of the divine process. When you surrender, God can really be effective in your life. If God provide for sparrows and lilies, He will certainly provide for you. Your Father knows every need. He has been there all along. Like the sparrows, "Open your mouth wide and allow God to fill it."

Since many things are lost in the process, the aftermath can seem frightening. Still, no matter how painful or unbearable, loss is considered gain and gain outweighs every loss. Attachments to certain people or things often remain in the sieve. Perhaps one of the greatest Christian writers ever, C. S. Lewis, says it the following way, "To experience great pain or to suffer great loss means that at some point there was an even greater love or joy." Lewis further said that "Given the opportunity to remove that person or thing, most would likely decline." Great memories never die. They remain in the heart.

Through "necessary losses," the courage to forge ahead is found. When you are sifted, the impact remains, but life really does go on. Great pain or great loss is indicative of an even greater love, joy, or privilege. From Lewis' perspective, nothing significant is ever really lost, because the mere experience was a blessing. During moments of joy no one complains, but when fate calls one to suffer, good times are quickly forgotten. When you are sifted, human nature will cause you to focus on present pain and despair instead of past happiness and future joy.

No pain means that you have never experienced the deeper love of a family member and the depths of despair at their passing. Not feeling pain means you have never enjoyed seasons of abundance to be overtaken with loss and ruin. Not feeling pain means that you have never enjoyed great health, soundness of mind and strength, to endure illness, pain or worse.

A painless life means you have never had a great love who left you to mend a broken heart. No pain means that you have never suffered the comforts of a lovely home threatened by instability and uncertainty. No pain means you never had a great dream and the sadness of it not being fulfilled; or worse, to begin and taste the joy of that dream to be overtaken with failure. Embrace your pain, it won't kill you, it will make you stronger.

There is a saying that "The loss of a friend is like that of a limb; in time the wound does heal, but you never forget the loss." In due season, you reap, heal, and get better. Hold on and allow the purification process to take its course. Healing does not come without pain. What you lose is never forgotten. Job was restored and gained double for his trouble. Peter became the rock, one of the greatest saints ever. God built a mighty church through him. He healed and delivered many people.

No matter how hard the season, certain things were off limits. So look at what you still have, not at what is no longer there. Like Moses, you may only see a staff, but you might be holding the rod to part your red seas. What is in your hand? Whatever you have is all God need to bless you. The seed God will use to bring forth your harvest. Whatever remains is the remnant, to rebuild and restore you.

In great despair, remember your emotions are the direct opposite of something greater that you once experienced. Embrace your pain. You did not run in the good times so do not run now. One reason the process is so hard is because you have lived, loved and been under God's grace before. You have first hand knowledge of His miracles. That is not easy to forget.

Remind yourself that sifting only occur with His permission. God does not take to just take away, but to restore better than you could ever imagine. Pain is often underestimated, but is perhaps the truest gage of a blessed life. You never really appreciate what you have until it is threatened. Real growth rarely occur without a painful season or two. Crisis is often the catalyst for great change.

Purification, though painful strengthens not destroys. Somehow you get through victoriously. A very wise Minister once said, "When you find your misery, you find your ministry." No light is brighter than a Christian refined in the fiery furnace of trial. No testimony is as intense or profound than one who survived the shakedown.

Your weakness positioned you to shine. Lives change because of it. Share your testimony. It exalts God. Remember the story is for His Glory. Like a metal smithy, the hottest heat was not applied to destroy you, but to bring out your brilliance. Now you can see what God has seen all alone—His reflection. You survived the shakedown. You are whole. Your faith withstood the test of a lifetime. You held on during the shakedown. Though bruised, broken, and brittle, your faith did not fail.

Chapter 7

Lessons from the Sieve

Some of the greatest lessons are learned from defeats not victories. Some battles cannot be fought or won, simply endured. Fighting won't change a thing. There is a point where stillness is required. When it is important to listen and move only when instructed. No man can fight or alter destiny, "What is ordained is ordained." When "the chips are down" or "the going gets tough," thank God, claim peace, and listen for direction.

There are always hidden lessons during trials. Within harsh trials are great lessons. When you master the challenge, you come closer to your divine purpose. Miss it and fate will bring the situation back to your doorstep in some new version. Mastering trials prepare you for future ones. That is the purpose of the process. Experience eases almost anything including sifting. In time, you will be sifted again, but only when you are in the midst of something greater than yourself. When faced with forks in the road, you will be certain you have heard from God.

Sometimes God intentionally gives a specific word that must be sifted. Never doubt His direction for your life. He is the source. When you are sifted, it is sometimes difficult to be thankful. Thank Him for sustaining your "this day." Be thankful for what you have, no matter how little. Be grateful for manna. It sustains. Manna or daily bread is all that is needed for God to meet your needs. Tomorrow's bread takes care of itself. Thank God for what you have today.

Count Your Blessings

Spencer Johnson said it best, "Yesterday is gone; tomorrow may never be; today is the only gift we have, and this is why it is called the precious present." Life is precious, a gift to be enjoyed in the moment. Learn the value of everything God has allowed in your life.

Live in the moment. No one is promised tomorrow. Count your blessings, and yes, name them one by one. When you are sifted, that technique will help to maintain your sanity. Gratitude is a blessing. When feeling blue count your blessings. "You will be surprised at what the Lord has done. Thankfulness often turns to praise, and praise gets God's attention.

The great writer Og Mandino, in his fabulous novel, *The Greatest Miracle in the World*, says "Count your blessings." Remind yourself of great things and stop dwelling on bitter ones. If you can see, hear, or smell, count your blessings. If you are in your right mind, count again. If you have someone to love and especially someone to love you back, keep counting. If you have clothes on your back, bread in your cabinet, my, aren't you blessed.

Are you healthy, devoid of sickness? Your numbers should be going higher. Have you lost a loved one, then you are blessed that God placed them in your life. Are you bankrupt, "broke, busted or disgusted," then you know the joy of having money and the things it can afford, another blessing? Are you homeless due to circumstances beyond your control? Then you are blessed with the memory of a home and the hope of building again.

If you are hungry, that means you are blessed to have known the delicacies of great food. Children in sub-Saharan Africa go without food for days or weeks, often dying from hunger. The scraps that are thrown away at the average American dinner table could sustain them. Even at your hungriest, you have probably never been near death and could get a meal somewhere if necessary, count again. Do you have at least one good friend then, you have found the greatest blessing of all.

When you are sifted, blessings are all around. You might have to look harder, but they are there. If you are reading this you are blessed with the ability to read, a gift many adults do not have. Stop looking at what you do not have, what you can not do and start focusing on your *cans*. Focus on joy, not pain, peace not chaos, abundance not lack; success not failure; love not loss; happiness not sadness; and, health not illness.

The great motivator, Napoleon Hill wrote, "Your mind creates and attracts circumstances and situations." In many ways that is true. Find negative, critical, unhappy, individuals and you will find despair and sub standard living. Sifting provide a better perspective of life.

Remember, the devil only posses the power he is given. Don't give him your mind. He operates best when you fear or waver. Think of Job and *Mrs. Job* and their losses. Then, think of how their story ended. You can be certain they both limped. At times, their scars could be seen, but in the midst of it they found great joy.

God is not some wimpy, can't get the job done, God. Nothing goes on in His universe without His knowledge. He knows every aspect of creation and the perfect time for your breakthrough. Even when you do not see Him, He is near. Sometimes He stands back His hand because there are some lessons you won't learn without adversity. Real success cannot be obtained independent of God. The smallest task is unsuccessful without Him.

He sits and waits for you to make right choices. All you need to do is call. In weakness, His strength is perfected. You are never too messed up that God cannot salvage you. He specializes in *pit situations*. If your situation is hopeless, beyond repair, you are a prime candidate for restoration, rejuvenation and supernatural favor. You are in the perfect place for a miracle.

God has given you a sound mind and is guiding you to things to alter your circumstances. He raised you to be a victor, not a victim. He knows you will master the lessons and graduate with honors. The enemy wants you to lose sight of God and focus on your problems. Don't ask God for signs ask for guidance. Signs could make you vulnerable to the enemy and further disrupt your course. Master each challenge and your trials will suddenly disappear.

Lessons from the Sieve

This Day

God Never Fails

Don't Limit God

Zero + God = Miracles

Time Changes Everything

Faith Works When You Work It

Worry Weakens Your Spirit

A Real Need Never Goes Unmet

Great Friends Do Give Awful Advice

Some Roads Must Be Traveled Alone

Prayer Powerfully Impact Outcome

Life Goes On… So Will Most People

Money Appears When It Is Most Needed

Believe God's Word Not Your Situation

"Faith Will Only Produce What Is

Trust God

Needs, especially daily ones are surprisingly met in unexpected and unique ways. Manna, the bread from heaven is the provisional blessing of those in the wilderness. God's mercy and grace are ever present. Whatever you are incapable of handling, He is over qualified to do. There is no job description He can not fill. God knows things about you that need adjusting, but would rather you realize them yourself. He wants you to accept who you are in Him. If that means eliminating old habits, friends, and yes, in some cases certain family members, so be it.

Dying to self is a privilege. It is the best gift you can give to yourself, but more importantly a gift you give to God. Sifting develop insight into the plight and challenges of your fellow sisters and brothers. No matter how hard the season, there are others who suffer worse. Trials force patience, and patience brings a harvest and the maturity to handle magnificent blessings.

Sifting is not a behind the curtain process. People will know you are going through something, although most won't be able to detect the inner turmoil. Don't expect them to understand it. When it is over, you will be in the position God want you to share your testimony. Then, they will know that your life has changed. In many ways you will be in a better position to choose who continue in your game of life. Sifting does that.

Be Thankful

You may have to look harder, but blessings are waiting to be noticed. Little things like getting through a day without a major catastrophe are welcomed blessings. Staying sane is a joy. The ability to purchase a favorite scoop of ice cream, coffee, or some other small treat is a blessing. Each gift great and small is wonderful. Sound mind, health, and strength are ultimate gifts. Those who have healthy, living, family members are blessed beyond measure.

Life is a treasure, a gift to be enjoyed by those who posses it. Appreciate God in everything. Focus on the pleasures and riches of His kingdom. There is a specified period to bring forth a harvest. Trust God's timing. When you are sifted, the remnants are enough for God to build, restore, and replenish a broken life. In most cases God will supernaturally intervene to rebuild what the devourer destroyed.

This Day

Whether you like it or not live in the moment. "This day" becomes the only one that matters. No matter how long the sifted season, it is just that, a season. And, seasons change. There are few who get through life without a visit in the sieve. The permitted time is that and when it is over, it is over. Solomon, the wisest man who ever lived, understood clearly that "There is a time and a season for everything under the sun." Don't rush the process. Allow God to perfect the harvest. How long, you ask, as long as it takes. If you endure, your change will come.

Focus

Don't miss the beauty of the season. Winter may be long, but spring will come. Don't lose sight of God's promises. Sifting produces faith and determination. No one will ever have to tell you about God's goodness, ability, or power, because you know them first hand. Walk by faith. Focus on the water walker--Jesus. You can lose anything or anyone and He will sustain you. Trust your spirit, not your circumstances. If you pay attention, your spirit will warn, guide, soothe, and inform you when the season is ending

Be Still

Spend time alone with God. Sifting draws you to Him. It increase, stretch, and strengthen you. When the enemy is near, you sense him. You don't have to resist him; he has to resist you. You are an heir with full authority, rights, and promises. God words are meat to your soul. Great faith is incomplete without testing. Great deeds cannot be accomplished without the process.

The "keys to the kingdom" are in your hands. Your words create new life and opportunities. You are a builder, restorer, and a repairer of your own broken life. Use what you learn to fulfill the great commission. When you encounter someone facing the trial of his or her life, let them know that Jesus never fails.

Don't Limit God

When you are sifted, you may lower your expectations of God. For example, *Lord, get me through the day* instead of, *God I want all the promises you have for me today.* You embrace crumbs and no longer desire the loaf of bread. Like the prodigal son, who forgot his divine connection to the Father, don't forget yours (Luke 15:11). When failure is before you, it is easy to forget that God has a great plan and purpose for your life.

When you confess, God freely forgives, for He gives to you that which you are unable to give yourself. He is the God of new beginnings. Do not limit Him, not even with your prayers. Be mature enough to mean "Thy will be done."

Do not manipulate your season. Let it take its course. God is qualified to deliver. Whatever you lack, He owns in abundance. He is not a one-time wonder God. He continues to do miracles, His specialty (Exodus 34:10). He is waiting for you to align your will with His. He is the great I Am. Whatever you need, fill in the "I Am," and He is. There is nothing God cannot do. Psalms 81:10, says, "Open your mouth wide and He will fill it." What do you lack; what have you been hoping for; what have you missed out on? Then trust the great "I Am" to provide.

Share the Story

Eyes have not seen what God does when you do not limit Him. His word says speak to your mountains. You better start talking, so they will move. Expect some rumblings to occur because you have the keys to the kingdom. You are an heir and when you bid according to your Father, it is so. Summon the miracles awaiting you. "Call those things that are not as though they are." Those lessons are a part of your testimony.

"Give Back"

Teach others about challenges and overcoming them. Hurting souls need to know that God never fails. Unwavering faith is not easy, impossible at time, but there is no option. "If you perish, perish believing God," Sifting is a faith adventure. No book or movie can compare. To get to the ending you must have unwavering faith. No one can see the ending except God.

If you controlled the story, it would not be as adventurous. Your version would probably be predictable. You would resolve crisis immediately to avoid pain, but God does not operate that way. Remember the disciples? Peter denied him and Thomas needed to see nail prints. At some point they all questioned their Lord. Still, Jesus was always there when they needed Him most. And, when He was no longer with them, He even left The Holy Spirit to comfort and guide them.

The disciples never matured to the point where they no longer needed God and His son, Jesus. They learned He is ever present, caring for them no matter what. A real need is never neglected. And, if money can take care of your problem then it is not that great compared to health, life or death matters. Survive it at all cost.

Don't expect anyone to understand. As hard as it might be, don't hold it against them. Friends and relatives give advice from their experiences and perspectives. Oh, they may be wise but they have not had your experience. As close as Job was to his friends, in the end, God spoke harshly and said they had spoken foolishly.

Those close to you may be the most difficult and least empathetic. They add despair by their inability to comprehend your problem. They are concerned and well meaning, but clueless. Those who have not walked in or near your shoes are presumptuous at best. Seek counsel from those who have been in and survived what you are going through.

Survival is a full time job. You cannot survive while being pulled down by others. You will have to keep some people at bay. They might be offended, but do not join forces with the opposition in the middle of a battle. Draw closer to God. Job's friends loved him no doubt and were well meaning. They just insisted he saw things from their perspective. They were certain that Job was guilty of something.

You have to know your position with God, His word, and how He has already operated in your life. Hold fast to any promises. Take Him, not your situation at His word. Whether those around you realize it or not, they are a part of what God is doing in your life. He is working something out in them too.

When God transforms your situation, everyone that needs to know, will know. He wants some head scratching, how did they do those conversations. He wants some there is no way they could have gotten through because I was there. He wants them to know and trust in His power. The story is for His glory. When you are at the end of your rope, He is there.

Pray

Prayer powerfully affects outcome. Pour your soul out to Him. "Tell him all about your troubles." After you tell him, praise Him. And, while you are down there, thank Him. Start with a specific number of blessings each day and add more, you will be surprised how much time you spend just thanking and praising Him. Thank Him for "this day." Another one is behind you. Thank Him and praise Him for the one to come.

Do not be anxious. Cast your cares, your Redeemer lives. Spend as much time as possible with Him. He is the only one that can change your situation. Don't waste time moping. Pity parties prevent you from hearing God's voice. Ask Him each day what He would have you do, and do it. Let Him bear your daily burden. Hr sustains you. God still grants miracles. There is no better time to experience them than when you are sifted.

Expect Miracles

Spiritual solutions conflict natural laws. When you are sifted, relying on natural methods is foolish when you are expecting a Godly outcome. Logic as known is illogical when you want a spiritual outcome. Spiritual solutions defy conventional wisdom.

God can do mind boggling things to alter your situation. If you are honest, many red seas in your life have been parted because of His miracle working power. Miracles are not just for a select few, but those who God want to shine through.

Challenges are significant for great change, embrace them. Do not run from them. Even though they create chaos and confusion, chaos is often a straight pathway to life altering change. It provides the opportunity to clean your spiritual, physical, emotional, and financial house. When life becomes too much, make necessary changes. You may have to rid yourself of some people, places and things, but the eternal benefit is well worth it.

Change is not always negative forces you out of your comfort zone. Change, in many cases is merely the opposite of the present state or the situation you want to get out of, to get to the place you are going. In science a substance is a substance no matter what. For example if you burn a piece of paper, the ashes are still parts of the original component. The original component is still paper, but in a different form, ashes. Beloved, you are like those ashes, still the same, but in a different form. Instead of running trying to find what was lost, accept your new state.

Run to Win

Stay in the race. There is too much at stake. Focus on God and you will find that anything lost is worth it. Had you not gone through the sieve, you would be impure, unholy, unworthy, and unprepared of the blessings now. Pain and broken dreams are a part of life, one that everyone would like to bypass; yet no one escapes.

Once you are sifted, never forget God's grace, mercy, and goodness. You might limp, but you will also receive your new name, Israel, Prince, and Inheritor. Or, whatever name God gives you—writer, entrepreneur, minister, teacher, etc. How much are you willing to give for a limp and some thorns?

Are you willing to trust and believe that whatever is ordained is ordained? Are you willing to believe that God does not allow suffering beyond what you can bear? Are you willing to believe He'll meet you at the finish line and place the crown upon your head? Then suddenly, you have mastered the lessons. Your river can flow again.

In many instances, you won't be able to pinpoint the exact moment, you will just know. Like the suddenlies, the end of the season is sudden and subtle. There will be a knowing that the worse is over.

You survived and God will grant you double for your trouble. Those who stayed are thrilled because they too are rewarded. You have been sifted and the cares of the world are just that. Nothing can ever shake you like that again. Even another "sifting" would not be as harsh because you have experience and survived! Survival is the key to enduring next time. You are a conqueror.

The glory is upon you. Everyone who sees you will know there is something about you. Your peace confounds human understanding. God has perfected your life. When you thought you were alone, Jesus was always there. He took the hardest punches on your behalf. He hedged you. You are in a new season of abundance, prosperity, and sweet rest, ready to bring fruit that last a lifetime.

Jesus was right. You made it. Your faith is stronger than ever. You are a bona fide survivor. You managed to stay in the race. The process seemed unending, but you made it to your destination. Welcome to the place that you fought to get to—Harvestime! Now you are beginning to see why your faith could not fail.

Chapter 8

Harvest Time

The season began with an onslaught of *suddenlies* that changed life as you knew it. No matter what things were like before, they will never be the same. *It* caused you to question everything. At times you thought you would lose your mind, but you didn't. You survived the test of a lifetime. All-Powerful met limited power and won.
"Time is out of the equation." Not enough is gone giving way to more than enough. Finally, it is harvest time! Oppression, depression, and hopelessness are over and new beginnings are on the horizon. The enemy gave it his best shot. It seemed as if he would win, but you and God remained the majority. Now you know that the battle was never yours to fight, but God's to win. The enemy's beef was never with you, but with Him.

You were merely a pawn in the midst of a greater divine scheme. When you felt like giving up God strengthened you. He was preparing you for unlimited blessings. He came so that you would live the abundant life you deserve. You understand sifting, the shakedown, and the sieve. At the appointed time, you arrived to your destiny, Harvest time.

You have been tried, tested and refined. The devourer no longer has permission to operate in your life. His reign of terror is officially over. He waged a fierce war, but time ran out. Former things are behind you. God has done a brand new thing. He restored you and gave you everything plus some extra stuff. Your faithfulness is finally rewarded.

As brittle as you were, you survived the shakedown. You made it through the sieve to the finish line. This is your kairos moment. The one mentioned earlier where time cooperates with your being. This is your time. This is your story. The ending is like a new beginning where favor does not cease. "It is a new season."

God is faithful, so faithful. You know that better than anyone. You are no longer a babe, but a mature, wise, saint, like Peter, you too are rock solid. Your foundation is strong. Even when you are sifted again, you will survive the next shakedown.

Now that you are out of the sieve admit it, you could not perceive your victory being so sweet. *They* are still talking, babbling, confused. *They* are still trying to figure it out. Some even want you to believe *they* knew you would get through the sieve. *They* watched closely, but could not comprehend how God would deliver you. *They* were certain that you could not deliver yourself.

They were not forced through the sieve, nor had the edge of the cliff experiences you had. Life was not drained from them as it was from you. In your hopeless, frail, and weak state, God saw your seeds and nurtured the magnanimous faith that cannot fail.

They still cannot figure it out. They don't know why you did not cave in to the pressure, crack up, give up, and leave defeated. They don't know how often you almost did.

By now, you certainly know the hope of God and "the misery you experienced is your ministry." Nothing will ever be the same. To gain something great, you must sometimes lose precious things. Lessons you may have never embraced, experiences you would have overlooked, are woven into the fabric of your character. You were bound in the fiery furnace, baked to a crisp, but came out without a hint of smoke.

You are wise, not worldly wisdom, but wisdom beyond anything you could imagine. From now own, you can never make a decision or face a crisis without Him.

Those lessons are a part of your history. They are memorial stones for the seasons ahead. They are survival guides to a better future. Your testimony will transform many lives.

You have the sweet smell of victory, but it did not come easy. You were kneaded, set aside to rise in preparation for the feast you now partake of. This bread is unlike any you have ever had, but came with a hefty price tag. You endured each stage. Now your bread is rich, delicious, and sustaining.

Once removed from the scorching oven, you cooled down before taking center stage at the banquet table. You are the star with top billing at the victory feast. Friends, enemies, doubters, naysayers, critics, or as today's slang goes, your haters have been waiting to see how your story ends, when you know it is only beginning. Even if they wished you harm, you would never know it. Everyone wants to sample the enduring, sustaining bread.

The feast is unlike anything you could imagine. Your very enemy is your footstool. Your challenges have been stepping-stones to greater things. God's goodness and mercy are the main course. Those seated at the table remain confused. What seemed foolish before remains a mystery, except now they applaud you. Like the story of The Little Red Hen, they all want "a piece." Hey, many think they are entitled.

That hardworking hen needed a little help but could find none during planting and harvesting. No one wanted to till the ground, plant seed, or pull wheat from the ground. Those around were unwilling to help knead bread or place it in the oven. They wanted to avoid the process. Not until the sweet aroma filled the air, did they "show up" ready for the feast. Unlike her, you know the feast is not only for you, but those aware of the process. By now they are bursting with curiosity. This is your opportunity to tell your story.

In the midst of the feast share the bread story. Most will overlook the process, but you never forget. They need to hear how you rose from near death to the blessed place you enjoy. The great poet Mayou Angelou says it in the following manner, "But still I rise." The implication is that no matter what happens, you will survive. Your perpetual thorn reminds you of the season. Others may not see it, but it is there. No one, except you will seem to remember planting, tilling, milling, or the purification process. All they will see is the final product, baked bread--your season of restoration, rejuvenation, and supernatural favor.

Now that is a party no one will want to miss. No matter who joins--friend or foe, you are obligated to share. They will never taste anything like it. To eat, they will have to hear the bread story and listen as you explain the main course. None of them could imagine the cost. They talked among themselves, but no one dared say anything to you. They said you were in denial, irrational, foolish, selfish, mad, but somehow you continued to believe God. They don't know how you survived because in their "heart of hearts," they would have perished. In their wildest dream, they could never envision themselves standing in the midst of the storms that raged your life, and certainly not surviving them.

At times they cheered hoping you would make it. Other times, they became envious of how and why you would not give up. Somehow, God continued to sustain you. So celebrate. Enjoy your new life and watch those who denied or questioned God's power, embrace Him. Everyone had to know about your journey. At times you wondered why it took so long. But God remained silently in the room waiting for you to complete the process.

Something explosive was happening. Your bread is not ordinary it is life, true manna, sustaining grace. Manna, the bread given to the Israelites to ensure they would survive the wilderness, sustained you. When the Israelites got more than a day's supply, they spoiled the blessing. You learned a valuable lesson. Do not store tomorrow's problems in today's blessings. Tomorrow may have challenges, but "today is a gift, a precious present." At times you questioned the manna, even came to dislike it, but it always met your need.

Like the Israelites you were excited at first that your needs were being met. After a while, manna became mundane, redundant. You wanted more than a this day blessing and began to wonder what was taking so long. Your insight about that bread has expanded to appreciate God's sufficiency. You had no control over any aspect of life. God had to deliver everything or you would have died. The thought that life was not in your hand is a humbling process. Everyone, no matter who goes to the grave the same way. You have insight about the meaning of "daily bread."

Blessings are like that, meeting now needs. You cannot retrieve them from the past nor store them for tomorrow. They are for today. The significance of bread is found in the following statement:

Workers who built pyramids in Egypt were paid in bread. A family of four could live 10 years off the bread produced by one acre of wheat. Assuming a sandwich was eaten for breakfast, lunch, and dinner, it would take 168 days to eat the amount of bread produced from one bushel of wheat.

Bread sustains and gives life. In order for Him to get the glory they had to see you survive. They could not hear you say, "I know my Redeemer lives," or "Though they slay me, yet will I praise Him." They wondered how you continued to serve a God who allowed such hardships.

Like Mrs. Job, they waited to see you curse God. They did not know that you felt cursed.

By surviving, you reap many benefits. Because of God's goodness, you have the power to sustain yourself. There must be a story or there is no glory. It was never anything you did, far from it. You were not cursed as you felt. Just when you thought satan was winning, God wove sustaining grace through your situation.

The devil messed with your mind, but the only power he had was the power you gave him. When you were weak, you gave him great power to increase his effectiveness. When you did not yield and trust God, the enemy created further havoc in your life. When you failed to remember that God created the enemy, you gave him even greater control. He needed permission to wreak havoc in your life. He thought enough of your potential to go directly to God for permission. He made a special request, which meant he knew something great was inside. He was after the seed. He did his best to destroy it before the process ended.

Because of his arrogance, the same pride that got him tossed out of Heaven, he must have forgotten that the battle was already won. God is faithful and did not allow you to be sifted to lose, but so that your victory would be complete. He wanted you to understand that when faced with trials He is your only source. That truth makes future siftings easier. When faced with similar or worse trials, believe that God knows all, is all-powerful, and all mighty. Do not try to comprehend His ways. Just accept His will. He has the perfect plan for your life.

God knew the lessons you had to experience before you could appreciate your new season. He had to remind you of the many blessings taken for granted. At any time, He could have stopped the process, but you were not ready. As difficult as it was to grant permission, He knew you needed to experience fall, winter, spring and finally, summer, where the harvest is plentiful. You have new purpose.

Like the bread that sustained you, the process was necessary. The broken bread perfected you in your weakness. You came to understand that "all things really are possible through Christ." Now that you are strengthened, you must lead your brothers to their blessed place. You can be a blessing because you are in a blessed position.

Your situation would have never worked without a bona fide, certifiable miracle. You know the key to obtaining them--survival and faith. You know that zero is the perfect place for God to make the greatest change of your life. You know that miracles can only happen in hopeless, helpless, situations. They have no rationale, rhyme, or reason. Zero can be an exciting place because it positions you for the final shakedown, where God is obligated to fulfill His Word. If there is still hope, an option, or the ability to resolve it on your own then you are not ready for a miracle. If not, ask Him for one. Be courageous and believe that even if your faith fails, God's compassion will not.

> *When Zero meets God expect a miracle*

God is not in the failing business. God can transform your circumstances in an instant and for a lifetime. He is the epitome of success. The same God who told Joshua, "If you meditate on my words, you will have good success." Not just success, because anyone can appear successful, but good success. Good success remains long after you are gone for your children and theirs to enjoy.

Perhaps the greatest benefit of sifting is the miracle of restoration. God personally rebukes the devourer for you. He wants everyone to see your blessings. The way that He restores is amazing. Man cannot understand it, wisdom cannot explain it, and logic cannot rationalize it. God restores in ways that are senseless in the natural. He literally gives houses you could never afford, land you don't own, healing for incurable diseases, jobs you are not qualified for, and money you did not earn. He gives new love, restores old, and places a divine vision in your heart. Most of all, He gives you peace, the thing that eluded you during the season.

Although everyone can be restored, not everyone is. Those who experience restoration wait and trust God. Those who do not forfeit or further delay their blessing with unbelief. Some do not experience restoration because they do not survive the shakedown. They give up. Remember, God grants free will. You must will yourself to survive. Those who do not experience restoration might blame God, but it is their own choice. No matter how difficult, Jesus prayed and the only way to fail is to give up.

Sadly, many get to the brink of harvest time and allow bitterness, anger, unforgiveness, rejection, fear, insecurities, paranoia, or the pressure of the sieve to prevent them from obtaining their harvest. They fail to realize that they are in the last stage, which is often the most difficult. They do not understand that all they need is to hold on and complete the process.

Harvestime is bittersweet because you can never forget the severity of the process. Still you accept the blessings you have. Time has a way of creating good memories out of bad ones. You have entered a season of peace, devoid of chaos and circumstantial living. Restoration gives you new focus. It gives you peace and joy like never before. You realize that cycles of life are merely that – a time and a season.

Like the Jobs, you may long for things from your past, but can never live there again. Like them you enjoy your double portion. New visions and desires are born. What was once impossible is now easy with God at the helm. There are real and spiritual connotations to how and what God restores. Remind yourself of the many ways He restores and mediate on what it means.

> **Restore**: *God gives back, returns, and recovers you from ruin or decay. He repairs; renew, replaces, and reinstates. He heals, cures, and revives. He replaces, recovers, reconstructs, reestablishes, and restores. God alone has the power to restore, renew strength, to provide vigor.*

Restoration is where lost things are found, perhaps not in their original state but available in some form. God gives new things. Things will just happen. You will be overwhelmed by the goodness of God. Blessed indeed will be an understatement. The favor of God is obvious in life. This is your time, your season to be blessed. Everyone wants blessings so people may ask, "How did you do that?" No matter what their opinions, they will want to know about the blessings.

It is time for you to testify to the goodness of God. They will want to hear your story, because they want what you have. When you were sifted, many negative circumstances, opportunities, and people came into your life. Now there are wonderful people and great opportunities. They are a part of restoration to assist in rebuilding your life. Like trials, they help you as you move toward your destiny. You won't believe how blessed you are.

You may have to remain silent about many things because you will not understand them. Besides, others will not believe them anyway. There will be a particular glow that no one will be able to miss. God repaired your broken, fragmented pieces. You are whole. He knew to be completely effective you had to complete the process. Suddenly, you faced a shakedown that tried to destroy you. Though frail, you were only broken where needed to learn about His strength.

If an illness was involved, you might experience miraculous healing capabilities. If financial, you will desire to give to those who are less fortunate. If you lost loved ones, God will equip you with skills to handle those losses. You may find new people in your life with similar qualities. God restores with a gentle, compassionate hand. You are more complete than ever.

God rebuilt you to suit His divine purpose. You passed "with flying colors." God is pleased. "Your faith did not fail." Now rejoice! When you pray, you know God hears and answers. Although you might doubt yourself, you never again doubt God. You are more than a conqueror who understands who you are, a survivor. How could you have lived without that assurance and security before? You have new awareness. Your mission is to serve and please Him. Those who cannot grasp that will not understand you. Your life and everything about it must reflect Him. You seek life beyond yourself. His will is your will.

He is concerned about every aspect of your life. He sustains guides and gives wisdom to endure. Consult Him, praise Him, and thank Him every day. Your faith has made you whole. God's supernatural power is in your life. Some will embrace it, others will not. That is okay. Pray that they experience the peace of living a pure life. That does not mean you are perfect, far from it, but it does mean your perspective altered. You made it. You have a story, a testimony, and the glory it brings.

Sifted saints are bridge builders and innovators. They confound the norm and operate in the exception. They see through supernatural instead of natural eyes. Sifted saints are tried, tested and true. They understand that when God gives a vision, He makes provisions. Sifted saints know that God is obligated to perform His word. They are certain that they will reap at the proper time. Sifted saints do not wonder if God, but when God. And, even when unsure of themselves, they are always certain of God.

Satan desired to sift you, but you made it. Suddenly, God's blessings are beyond your greatest imagination. Tell the story and please tell it well. Don't be embarrassed about the discomforts of your season. Those tidbits, the unbelievable parts are the best part of your testimony.

Fail to tell the story and you fail to share the glory. Don't allow others to assume that your abundant living came without a price. Let the world know the cost of living a life for Christ. Most will not be able to look and tell what you survived unless you tell them.

Tell them about the Mrs. Job moments when you felt like giving up. Tell them that God saw your strength; the seed He knew was inside. Show them your limp and your thorn. Your name is on the walls of faith (Hebrews 11) along with other faithers like Abel, Enoch, Noah, Abraham, Sarah, Hannah, Joseph, Joshua, Moses, Daniel, Elijah, and the rest of those great men and women who served and trusted God in their hopeless states.

Somehow you stayed in the race. In the midst of it and in spite of it you held on and made it to the finish line. God positioned you to be victorious. Start thinking like God and acting like Jesus did when he walked the earth. You are commissioned, stripes earned to save in your sphere of influence. You are obligated to be understanding, caring, and kind. You have passed the test. Rejoice it is your season.

Satan desired you, but you have mastered every lesson and passed every test. All powerful was always in control. Time ran out. You survived and you make it to your destiny. You kept a seed, the one needed to bless you. You survived. Now exhale and embrace your future. Whatever it was, you survived. It did not overtake you. It did not destroy you. It did not drive you mad. And, it certainly did not kill you! It did not even rob you of your seed. It made it blossom more. It was what you needed to experience God's sustaining power in your life. Now that you have been sifted, your light shines. And, suddenly, you are blessed beyond anything you could imagine. Welcome to you final destination. You have arrived. It is Harvestime.

Dear One, if you are reading this, there is so much in store for you. If you are at zero, I have great news for you. You are finally ready for a miracle. Though bruised, broken and brittle, trust God even when you do not trust yourself. He knows exactly what is necessary to get you to your blessed place. Your faith might be weak but it will not fail.

Surviving the shakedown requires total faith and trust in God. You were not set apart for destruction, but for greatness. In the midst of your challenges continue to look for provisional blessings. Manna is always present. Suddenlies can only destroy you if you let them. So, get up, stop that pity party and fight for your life. Nothing is too hard for God. His strength is perfected while you are hopeless. Trust God for the outcome, I can assure you that God never fails.

Baby,
  This is the last draft (probably not 😊). Thanks for your support. You are one of a kind, a gift, a blessing from God. I thank God for ordaining our friendship and never allowing a break. I can't say you've changed much since 13!! You are still bossy, picky, greedy, sunny, loving, loyal, consistent, faithful and popular.

  No, really (all above is true), I thank God for you always. I don't know what I did to deserve you but I'm glad God saw it. And now I go on the official record…. I really am your best friend, #1, Uno, before you met anyone else, except Chris! (Ha hahahaha)

Cynthia
2007

Cynthia Curry is the founder of *Image Builders*, a non-profit development company. She is a Certified Grants Specialist, National Grants Reviewer and a member of "Who's Who Among Executives and Professionals." She is a gifted facilitator, speaker and planner. Her passion is reaching those who have lost hope and encouraging them to never give up. Mrs. Curry is married with two exceptional children, her pride and joy. She considers the assurance of her salvation as the greatest gift she has ever received.

Contact the author at imagebuilders.1@netzero.net.

To purchase and for additional information go to www.trafford.com/05-2199.

ISBN 1412073104-9